Technical Analysis for Beginners

Stop Blindly Following Stock Picks of Wall Street's Gurus and Learn Technical Analysis

Follow Koonitz:

www.koonitz.com

Twitter: @JumpyStocks

Published by Tripod Solutions Inc.

Book and Cover design by Koonitz

ISBN: 9781520110042

Second edition: March 2017

2

TABLE OF CONTENTS

INTRODUCTION

The other day, I was chatting with a friend and he told me a story similar to the one I had heard several times before. A young man had placed all his savings, about $20,000, on a single stock, after the advice of his father. The latter had mentioned that Affimax could not do anything but go up because the stock had already lost 50% of its value.

On November 17, 2012, Affimax indeed reached a high of $27.74. On February 13, 2013, the stock closed at $16.91. On February 14, the stock fell 31% at opening to $11.60, but it bounced back and closed at $15.74. That same day, in the morning, the well-meaning father advised his son to invest in that stock because he thought that it had reached an incredibly low limit, and it would only bounce back up from there. The son invested the $20,000 following the advice of his father at an average cost of $15.35 per share, for a total of 1,300 shares.

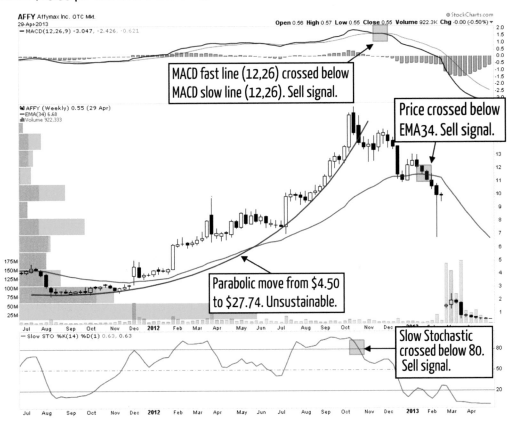

Figure Intro.1 Bad call. Chart courtesy of StockCharts.com

From February 15 to 22, 2013, the stock remained rather stable at $16.36. On February 25, following the weekend, the massacre happened. The stock fell violently and closed at $2.42, with the young man registering an unbelievable loss of $16,809. On April 18, the value of his investment was $1,326, compared to an original investment of $20,000.

Even the best technical analyst couldn't predict that one of the company's drugs would lead to the death of three patients. The product was pulled out of the market and the stock lost 85% of its value in a single day. This exceptional situation brings out an important element: too many investors blindly take the advice of their friends, their gurus or those close to them, without having any knowledge about their investment.

Who Can be Trusted?

This book does not intend to prevent you from trying the many stock market gurus you can find across the web. We can't deny that it may be interesting to follow the recommendations of a guru. Many are well connected with the market. Some of them have the flair, while others have research teams that do the technical work. However, you should know that a large number of those gurus have only very slight knowledge about technical analysis. Many of their recommendations are based on simple impulses or on fundamental stock analysis.

For a short- and medium-term investor, the fundamental analysis has very low importance. The fundamental analysis allows you to evaluate a company through accounting, financial and strategic analysis, which can rank it in comparison to its competitors. It also allows evaluating the development perspective according to market forces such as supply, demand and technological innovation. Fundamental analysis is more suitable for those who have long-term objectives, wishing to build a stable investment portfolio.

Many gurus spend their days in front of their screens. Often enough, their strategy consists of searching for a small gain from $250 to $300, for an investment of $5,000 to $10,000. As soon as they are positioned, they announce the new selection to their subscribers. As you cannot be connected in real time to their transactions, you cannot obtain the return that the "masters" obtain. We believe you can't win by using this strategy.

There's another point worth considering. Starting from the moment they announce their picks to their subscribers, some gurus are ready to sell what they've just recommended as a good buy. It's the same for the big banks. Their specialists provide us with recommendations, some of them quite questionable, which begin to resemble a marketing campaign.

More than anything, this book intends to allow newbie investors to assimilate some knowledge that will come in handy when it's time to buy or sell a financial stock, based on technical analysis of a chart. Trusting the advanced knowledge of a trading guru might be useful, but you should always do your homework and take a look at the chart of the stock suggested. Stay away from pump-and-dump schemes.

And you, what type of investor are you? What inspires you? Is it the day trading, the swing trading or the long-term investment? If you still want to choose a guru, it is up to you to find one who corresponds to your trading style and your availability. You may want to do day trading, but if you work during the daytime, forget it! Choose a guru who works in harmony with your trading style and your lifestyle.

When you shop for a new vehicle, you take the time to examine the various products offered to you. You do some research, look at magazines and do some road tests. It's normal when you're investing $30,000 in a vehicle. So why not do it when you invest on the stock exchange?

The beginning of my introduction has demonstrated something very important: it's necessary to avoid blindly trusting a colleague, a friend or a member of your family when it's time to invest in a financial stock. So, be careful when choosing your guru. Before trading, analyze the guru's recommendations to see if they seem to be quality ones. If your guru is safe, he will suggest good stocks every week. In that case, there's no need to run.

Make your own research

You should do some research for each financial stock before investing. To help you with your research, we strongly recommend Yahoo! Finance, which offers all the necessary information for the analysis of your stock. Here is the minimum information you need to get:

- The ticker of the company
- The sector of the company
- The stock market capitalization
- The number of employees
- Its competitors
- The high and low for the current year
- The date of the next release of quarterly results
- The American, European and Asian market trends

We are not minimizing the importance of a guru, but instead recommending that you understand and master technical analysis before anything else. It's the only way to validate the picks suggested by your specialist. You should always do the technical analysis of the stock you want to buy, in order to see if it's in good shape. All the examples of this book are based on past situations and are well documented. This book requires little technical knowledge. It addresses newbie investors who want to get to the heart of the matter faster.

It's time to start!

CHAPTER 1 – WHAT IS TECHNICAL ANALYSIS

Technical analysis is nothing more than the graphic representation of a financial stock, which highlights its strengths and weaknesses by using various indicators. Some websites even allow adding lines, drawings and comments in order to make a better presentation of a stock's trend and its support and resistance zone. Be aware: indicators do not foretell the future. They can help anticipate it through some patterns. After gaining experience, you will know how to anticipate certain actions of the market.

Before investing in a stock, it's vital to understand the information contained in a chart in order to be able to make the best investment decisions. It's similar to what you do when it's time to buy a computer or a tablet. You examine the technical features. You make comparisons between the different products in order to make the best decision.

You also must learn to read the information contained in a stock chart. A stock chart is the graphic representation of a stock price in a time frame divided into different types of periods: minutes, hours, days, weeks, months, quarters, etc. A stock chart presents a lot of information about price fluctuation, as well as the trading volume. Furthermore, it's also possible to add a lot of indicators, each one as distinct as the other.

Here is a list of free stock chart providers:

- Barchart
- Big Charts.com
- Free Stock Charts
- Google Finance
- StockCharts
- Stock Technical Analysis
- Trading View
- Yahoo! Finance

Type of Charts

There are several ways of representing stock prices. We can use the Open-High-Low-Close (OHLC) chart, the candlestick chart, the line, the dot, the area and many others. Here are three usual ways of showing the evolution of a stock price in a short period of time.

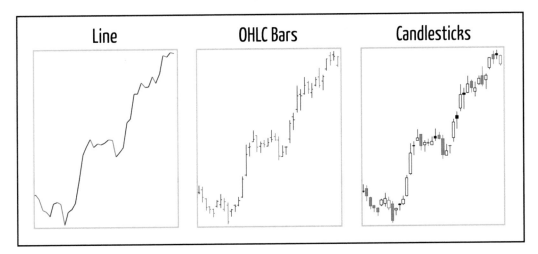

Figure 1.1 Type of charts.

The first chart format is a simple line. The only information found on this basic chart is the closing price for each time unit. Charted together, a large number of units takes the shape of a curve; this is most often used for a long-term chart.

The second format is the Open-High-Low-Close (OHLC) bars. It's a bar chart used to illustrate the movements of a financial stock in time. Each vertical line on the chart represents a time unit, for example, a week, a day or an hour. Each time unit is represented through an up-and-down shaft and two small horizontal traits. One to the left represents the price at the opening of the markets. The other to the right represents the price at the close of the markets.

The third format, the Japanese candlestick chart, presents the same information as the OHLC graph, but it has other advantages. Reading is simpler and faster. Note the similarity between the OHLC and the candlesticks. When the upward phase of the stock begins, there's an important space between two bars and two candlesticks. This space is called GAP and is often seen as a sign that announces a beautiful increase. This information is essential for the investor and is missing from the first format.

Candlesticks in Detail

The Japanese candlestick chart has been used for hundreds of years by Japanese retailers. This style of drawing the exchange rate of rice in one day has been simply applied to better interpret the price of a stock. It's pleasant-looking and shows clearly all the information required to analyze each trading day.

For the purposes of this book, we will focus on the Japanese candlesticks that provide the most complete information and which are by far the best expression of a stock chart. Figure 1.2 illustrates in detail a positive and a negative day on the stock market. According to the platforms we've used, a positive day will be represented through a white or green candlestick, and a negative day will be represented through a red or black candlestick.

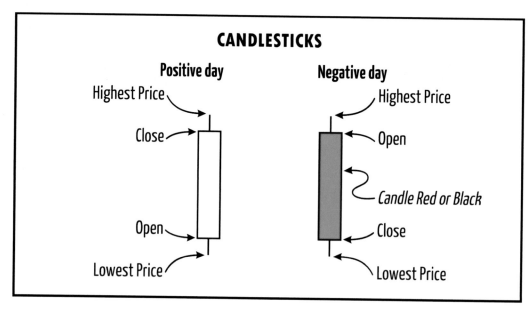

Figure 1.2 Japanese candlesticks.

The rectangular bodies represent the interval between the opening and the closing of a transaction period. The two fine black traits, called shadows, represent the extreme levels of the day. These traits are missing when the opening or closing of the price is made at one of its extremes.

The candlestick's length shows the strength that separates the lowest and the highest price. When the candlesticks for some days are shorter, there is a common ground between the bulls and bears. The only fault we could find is that its representation allows displaying smaller periods of time compared to others. Its width is greater than the OHLC chart.

When the closing level is getting nearer to the highest price of the day, this indicates that the buyers have taken control. A positive start can be foreseen for the next morning. When the closing level is getting nearer to the lowest price of the day, this indicates that the sellers are getting rid of their stocks. A negative start can be foreseen for the next morning.

We can count around a hundred candlestick figures or setups which offer clues about the future direction of stock price. A few figures are presented in **Chapter 10**. Many works have been written in this field. Feel free to read them to perfect your knowledge.

CHAPTER 2 – THE TREND

A key element in the technical analysis of a stock is to determine the stage the stock is in. This step is essential. It's very reassuring to know you have just invested in a stock that is going through a favorable period. Stage identification allows you to establish whether the stock is bullish, bearish or in a consolidation period.

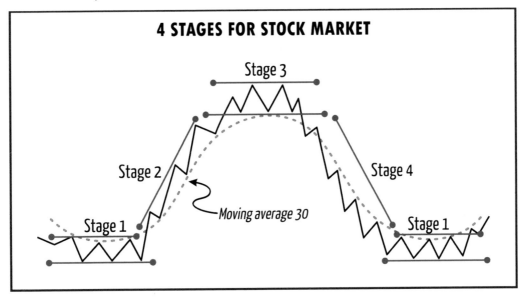

Figure 2.1 Four stages for stock market.

Look at these stages as the four seasons where the temperature levels swing back and forth from day to day to form a cycle. The temperature goes up in the spring, becomes steady at a high level in the summer, decreases in the autumn and becomes stable at a low level in the winter. Here are the stages to consider.

Stage 1

The foundation or consolidation stage: purchases and sales are balanced. The volume decreases. The market is reasonably stable. The moving average flattens. The stock price faces resistance. At the end of this first stage, the volumes should increase and the prices should position on the moving average.

Stage 2

The ascent stage: The best moment to buy occurs when price crosses above the moving average 30 periods (30-period SMA). The breakout of Stage 1 occurs on rising volumes. The beginning of Stage 2 is seen as a series of price increases, which could be jerky, with no significant lows and fixed by higher volumes. The demand is supported by the buyers, who do not want to miss the rally.

Stage 3

The ceiling stage: The share price enters into a re-balancing period. The latecomers buy, and the pros sell their shares. We get back to a balance between the selling and the buying-related price. It's an irregular market where new highs can be reached. Volume could be lower. The SMA30 flattens and falls below the stock price.

Stage 4

The breakdown stage: The sellers take the lead. The prices are below the SMA30, which begins to bend. The share price tends to decline quickly during the break. Regularly, we see an increase of the volume. It can be a slow agony or a severe drop.

Your investment strategy has to be different from one stage to the other. It can be difficult to detect the beginning and the end of the stages. This is why you should use a Simple Moving Average of 30 periods (SMA30) or an Exponential Moving Average of 34 periods (EMA34). When the stock price crosses this average, it should be considered a stage change. There is an intersection with this moving average at the beginning of Stage 2 (bullish) and in early Stage 4 (bearish).

Figure 2.2 Cirrus Logic and Stages. Chart courtesy of StockCharts.com

Figure 2.2 shows the four stages in a weekly format for Cirrus Logic, which staggers for a three-year period. It's always recommended you identify the stages by using a weekly chart. Daily charts offer too much volatility, which makes it more difficult to identify stages properly. The purchase of a share should be made at the beginning of Stage 2, and the sale should be made at the beginning of Stage 4.

The Trend

The trend concept is relatively simple. The trend defines the direction of stocks or markets. The trend may be positive or negative. A market may go up or go down, and it happens frequently to see a market without any trend, as if it were at a standstill. This type of market occurs when buyers and sellers agree on a price. You should always invest in the trend's direction. You should never go against the wave and try to guess the trend reversals. The market will take you back on the right way quickly. A stock with a confirmed positive trend will produce significant profits. Always sell when a trend reversal occurs.

The trend line

The trend line is the most under-estimated element in technical analysis. However, the simple fact of showing the direction and the momentum of a stock can be enough to establish our investment strategy. The direction can result in the increase or the decrease of the share's price. The momentum can be translated as the strength of the inclination of this trend. The trend line is an extremely uncommon tool on which you have full control. Among other things, it allows you to predict the trend reversals likely to occur, either positive or negative. No mathematical formula is required.

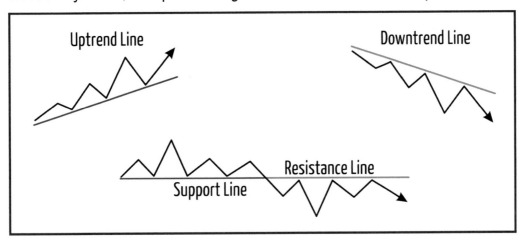

Figure 2.3 trend lines.

We can consider three types of trend line: the uptrend line with a positive slope, the downtrend line with a negative slope and the trend line with no slope, which is, in fact, a support or a resistance line. To be valid, the trend line has to be drawn so that it touches at least three candlesticks.

The higher the number of candlesticks, the more significant the trend line. When the trend is upward, the trend line has to be drawn so that it connects the base between the candlesticks. When the trend is downward, the trend line has to be drawn so that it connects the top between the candlesticks. The breaking of a trend line does not mean that a new trend has begun. It can be a false signal.

Uptrend Line

The uptrend line is helpful because it provides an upcoming indication of a downward exit point. This line looks like an increase. Some of them are abrupt, while others are scarcely tilted. The uptrend line represents a form of support with an upward trend. To be valid, the uptrend line has to be touched at least three times by one of the candlesticks, and it has to be drawn below the candlesticks. The break of this trend line sends the signal of a possible trend reversal. It's time to think about selling your stocks if your investment horizon is short-term.

Figure 2.4 Dow Jones and Uptrend line. Chart courtesy of StockCharts.com

The Dow Jones indicator in figure 2.4 shows four positive trends as well as four reversals. When a breakdown appears, an increase in volume is not required. However, the increase in volume may be felt if the stock loses value quickly and panic sets in on the market. The abrupt slope of a trend line would have more probabilities of breaking fast, because the support wouldn't have the time to be put in place.

Downtrend Line

The downtrend line provides indications of an upward exit point. The strength of this decline may fluctuate: some of them are steep, others are barely tilted. The downtrend line is a kind of resistance with a downward trend. For the downtrend line to be valid, the candlesticks must touch it at least three times. After gaining some experience, you will notice that all the investors become agitated at the same time when a breakout or a breakdown occurs. You are not the only one who has foreseen the breaking zone of a stock. Many other traders have noticed it. You have to act fast in order to maximize the opportunity that is being offered to you.

The volume must be upwards so that the break becomes relevant. To be valid, the breakout of a downtrend line must be made complete through volumes that are three to five times the average volume of the last 30 periods. The rising break represents a buy signal. From this point forward, buyers assume control of the marketplace.

Figure 2.5 Canadian Solar and Downtrend line. Chart courtesy of StockCharts.com

Canadian Solar has been dealing with a succession of downtrends, as the solar market has been losing its power of attraction since March 2014. Pay attention to three breaking points; each represents an excellent opportunity to purchase the stock.

Support and Resistance

Support and resistance are quite easy to master, and are features that must be part of your tool box. Above all, don't underestimate the importance of the support and resistance, which are essential to master technical analysis concepts. They represent the marking levels that buyers and sellers recognize and that make them act in consensus. Figure 2.6 shows a graphic representation of a security whose price runs into resistance and support. Make use of discipline by drawing lines of support and resistance, and you'll come out a winner. By mastering these levels, you can predict future rebounds.

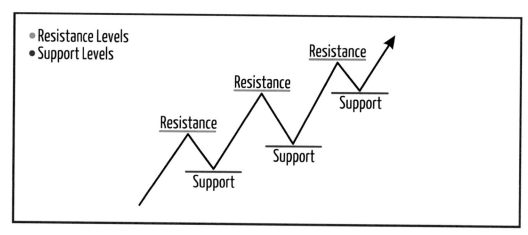

Figure 2.6 Support and resistance.

The support is a zone that the buyers find attractive. In this zone, the buyers dominate and push the market up. On the other hand, the resistance is a zone where the sellers dominate and therefore, they push the market down.

The support represents the lowest level where the share price could bounce. Demand is firmer than supply, which prevents the stock from collapsing below the support. The more the support zone is tested, the stronger it will become. The longer the support period, the more solid it will become.

However, the time wears out and the support will eventually decline. Some investors will give up, and they will be replaced by brand new investors who won't work with the same markers as the previous ones. The resistance and support stages evolve in time, according to the new reality of the financial markets.

There is a tendency to draw the support with one line only, and it's very good to do it like that. Nevertheless, a support should have a certain thickness. The wider the candlesticks' range as a support zone, the greater the margin of error in evaluating possible rebounds will be.

To make a better evaluation of the support zone, take the time to analyze the stock in a weekly format. The zone might be different, and you might reach the conclusion that changing the entry and exit targets is required. The support evolves according to the stock price. Volume fluctuations also lead to a variation in the stock price at different levels of trade.

Figure 2.7 Netflix and support zone. Chart courtesy of StockCharts.com

The above figure shows that Netflix has bounced back five times on the support zone within a year. If the downward break of the support happens, the stock can continue to decrease as long as brand-new support and fresh buyers are missing.

The resistance refers to the level the stock price could hit during the surge of a stock price. The sellers do not believe in a higher level and cash in their profits when the stock price touches the resistance. These are two opposing strategies.

While the crowd believes in a breakout, the pros sell when the stock price faces the resistance. The demand is simply not strong enough to cause an upward break. The pros take advantage to do a short sale and pocket the losses of the buyers who believe they are buying at the right time.

Like the support zone, the longer the resistance zone is, the stronger it will become. Additionally, use the weekly chart to validate the long-term resistance. The more the resistance is tested, the stronger it will become.

This means that many investors have extrapolated a break which was late and which brought in other investors to give it a chance. The more the resistance is tested, the more likely it is the break will cause a significant rise.

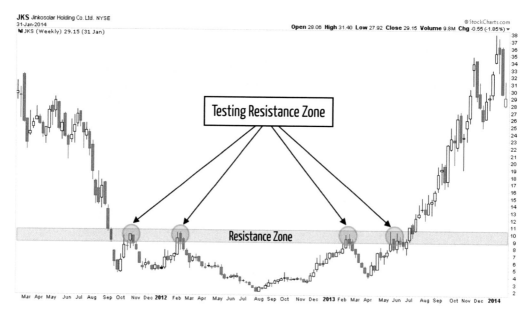

Figure 2.8 Jinkosolar Holding and resistance zone. Chart courtesy of StockCharts.com

Jinkosolar Holding suffered an outstanding drop from July to October 2011. Since then, the stock has touched its resistance of $10 several times, which led to a major resistance. When this resistance zone is clear, it will turn into a support zone.

Support and resistance zones evolve in time. A resistance strength with a limit of $3.00 for a stock will not be the same next month. The market evolves day by day, with old investors giving way to new ones.

The case from below shows American Reprographics and a support zone which turns into a resistance zone. Support at $4.00 has been tested several times. It also broke during the mini-crash of October 2011. The stock price has come back to test the support zone between August and October 2011, to break through finally in November 2011.

The stock price stumbled again over this support from July to September 2012. In early November 2012, the support zone collapsed and the stock lost half of its value in less than two months. The support zone has transformed into a resistance.

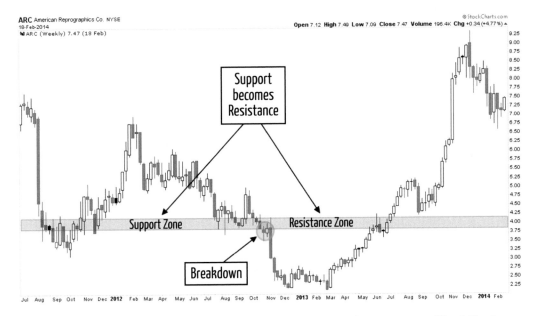

Figure 2.9 American Reprographics and support & resistance. Chart courtesy of StockCharts.com

Trend Channel

The trend channel draws its origin from the trend line, to which is added a parallel line to form a corridor. A trend channel looks like a rectangle in which the stock price bounces back many times between its upper and lower limits.

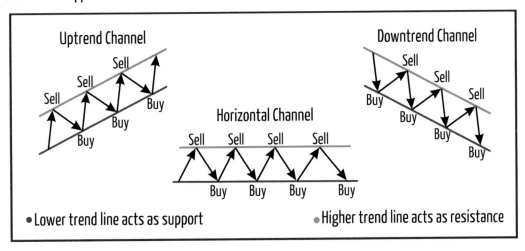

Figure 2.10 Channel. As the trend lines, we count three trend channels or corridors: an uptrend channel with a positive slope, a downward channel with a negative slope and a trend channel with no slope.

The top red line represents the resistance, and the lower green line represents the support. The way of treating the rebounds on resistance and on support is identical to one of the trend lines. The stock price stumbles over the resistance line and remains within the trend channel. The same happens with the support line: the stock price stumbles over the support line and remains within the trend channel.

> TACTICS – TREND LINE AND CORRIDOR. A trend line is a straight line which, to be meaningful, must touch the base or the top of candlesticks at least three times. The use of the trend line or channel allows anticipating the purchase and sell levels. The longer the line is, the stronger the breakout will become. The resistance is the level where the stock could stumble over during the increase of the share's price. The support refers to the level on which the stock price rebounds during the decline of the share price.

Divergence

Divergence can be defined as a difference, an opposition, or a contradiction between two elements. The concept of divergence remains quite simple, but many people have difficulty mastering it. Using indicators often highlights the divergence between the stock price and indicators. There are divergences or contradictions because the indicator does not move in the same way as the stock price.

There are two types of divergences: the upward or positive divergence and the downward or negative divergence. An upward divergence occurs when the indicator is up and the stock price is down. Usually, it's followed by an interesting boost in the share price.

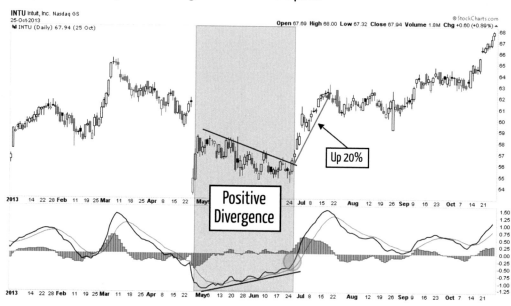

Figure 2.11 Intuit and positive divergence. Chart courtesy of StockCharts.com

The MACD indicator was added to the chart of Intuit Company. The gray area represents the upward divergence zone. The MACD is up, while the stock price is down. At the end of this zone, the stock price makes a steep increase and gains almost 15% in less than a month. The positive divergence allows the investor to see the potential increase, which is about to start. Put aside the stocks that present upward divergences and take action when the stock passes above the downtrend line.

Conversely, a downward divergence occurs when the indicator is down, and the stock price reaches a new high. It's quite possible that a dip in the stock price might appear, but this doesn't occur automatically. It can give a false signal. In case of doubt, restrain yourself and pass to another stock.

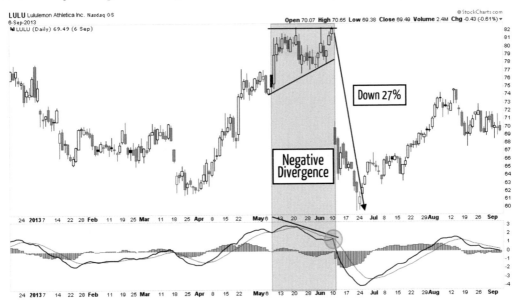

Figure 2.12 Lululemon and Negative divergence. Chart courtesy of StockCharts.com

The weekly figure of Lululemon Athletica shows a perfect bearish divergence. The MACD indicator is declining while the share price continues to grow and finally falls more than 27%. The negative divergence allows the investor to anticipate the possible decrease which is about to be triggered. Put aside the stocks that have downward divergences. If you are looking for a long-term investment, wait for the drop to end before buying.

CHAPTER 3 – TREND LINE BREAK

In the previous chapter, we discovered the importance of tracing the trend lines and channels. The method is simple and requires no calculation, just observation. The most important element brought by drawing these lines is the ability to provide landmarks in the projection of a future upward or downward break. The trend line break signals that the trend has just changed direction. It may be time to take action by selling your shares or by purchasing the coveted stock.

Breakout

A breakout occurs when there is a break of a resistance. This break has to be accompanied by a significant volume increase that must be three and five times the average volume of the last 30 days. Many small investors base their trading strategy on the break of a major resistance. The figure below shows the basic patterns of a breakout. It can occur during a positive trend, during a consolidation period or during a downward trend. Often, the stock takes a pause after the breakout and then tests the support zone before continuing its increase. This scenario is represented through the dotted lines.

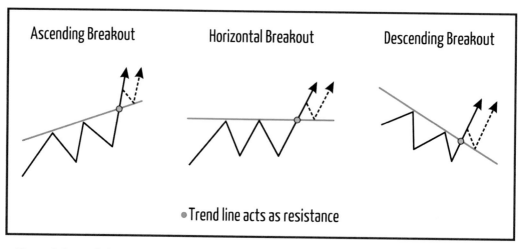

Figure 3.1 Upside breakout.

This strategy remains one of the most famous. However, you should consider that an important number of signals remain invalid. In fact, professionals have understood that many investors target these levels and take advantage to sell when the breakout is about to occur, so you end up getting a fake signal.

A true breakout needs some specifications to be valid. Foremost of all, there is a fairly long consolidation period preceding the breakout. Why? We have to give the stock time to build a good resistance, which, once surpassed, will become a strong support. Let's take the example of a breakout that happens after a period of consolidation of five days. It's likely that the stock should return below the resistance because the support generated like that would be too weak to contain the future sellers who may want to get rid of the stock.

Second, the resistance needs to be tested a few times in order to be recognized. The more the stock stumbles over a resistance, the stronger it becomes. Identify the stocks that have a consolidation of 20-30 periods. The base will be solid, and the stock's explosion will be much more vigorous. Third, the most important element concerns the volume. Obligatorily, the volume has to be three to five times higher than the average volume of the last 30 periods. This factor is crucial, and it validates the upward break.

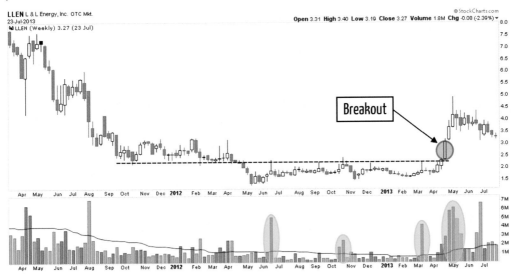

Figure 3.2 L&L Energy and breakout. Chart courtesy of StockCharts.com

Pay attention to the volume level following the upside breakout of L&L Energy in early April 2013. Rising volume propelled the stock from $2 to $5 in less than three weeks. This volume increase is more than three to five times higher than the average of the last 30 periods, represented by the blue line in the volume window. The accumulation period between May 2012 and April 2013 allows creating significant gain.

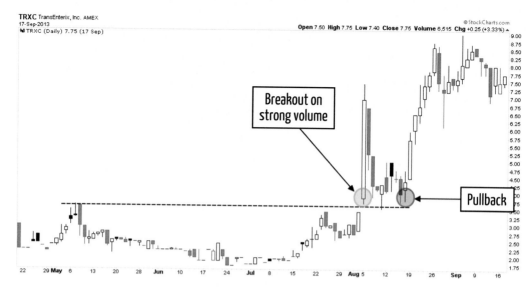

Figure 3.3 TransEnterix and Breakout. Chart courtesy of StockCharts.com

TransEnterix made an extraordinary breakout at the beginning of August 2013. The stock more than doubled in a single session. You missed that breakout? There's no need to worry. The stock comes back to test its support zone four days later, before pursuing its crazy ride.

This pattern following a resistance breakout frequently occurs. Never chase a stock. Place that stock on your watchlist. Wait two to three days to see whether it's testing the support zone again. Keep in mind that a stock will always make a downward correction, no matter the strength of the upward break. If not, pass to the next one. Opportunities are there every day.

Breakdown

In contrast to the breakout, the breakdown occurs when there is a downward break of the support zone. The breakdown is caused when many investors have lost confidence in their stock for various reasons. This loss of confidence may be caused by the poor trend in the sector, bad economic news or other information that might affect the stock. Some congestion occurs before the break, similar to when workers hit a wall with a mass in order to break it. Because of the pressure applied at the same location, the wall will ultimately crumble.

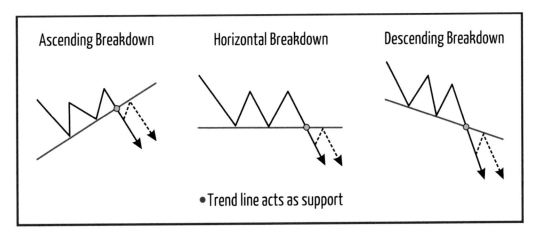

Figure 3.4 Breakdown.

Figure 3.4 illustrates the basic form of a breakdown. It can happen during a positive trend, a consolidation period or a downward trend. Unlike the breakout, the breakdown does not need a volume increase in order to be valid. A volume increase directly leads to a faster decline of the stock.

The downward break of an important support zone leads to a significant drop of the share. The breakdown is characterized by a total disinterest in a stock. It follows numerous attempts to break support. The strength of the support is proportional to the number of bounces.

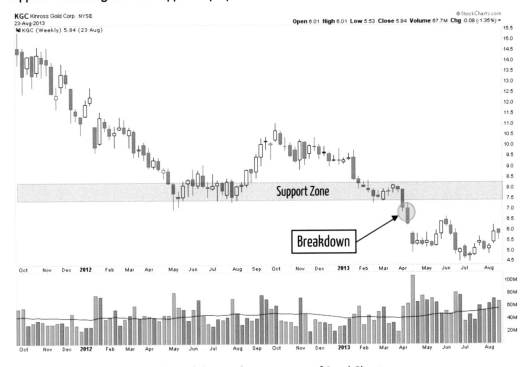

Figure 3.5 Kinross Gold and Breakdown. Chart courtesy of StockCharts.com

Look at the above chart for Kinross Gold. Between May and August 2012, there were numerous rebounds on the support zone. The buyers trusted in an upward return, and this is what happened. The stock gained more than 30% in two months. Consequently, the support zone was been tested again and collapsed in April 2013.

Notice the volume increase during the downward break. Shareholders abandoned the stock massively, creating panic. As mentioned earlier, the volume increase is not required during a breakdown. If there is one, the disruption will be even more efficient.

Channel Break

As we saw earlier, the trend channel is made of two parallel lines within which the stock price bounces back many times. The channel can be bullish, bearish or without any slope. We must realize that a stock in a positive trend channel can break upward of the upper line of the channel, or it can go under the lower line of the channel. Securities move as bullish or bearish cycles. Let's take a closer look at the breaks that occur in the opposite direction of the trend channel.

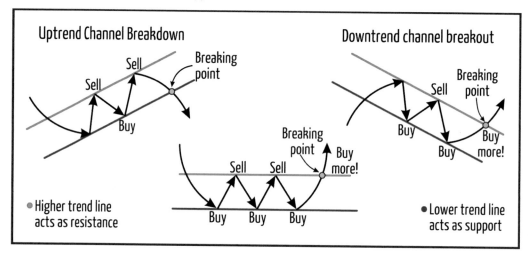

Figure 3.6 How to trade a Channel Breakout.

The above figure shows how to play the break of an upward trend channel, a downward trend channel and a consolidation period break. These models allow investors to anticipate a break with a significant impulse of the stock price. Get used to drawing your lines and trend channel, and your performance will register a solid increase.

Sell Short

In contrast to the market in general, many professionals use the trading strategy of short-selling the securities that are experiencing the breakdown. Without elaborating further measures, short-selling involves selling a stock that you do not possess, which will be bought at a cheaper price. This is the opposite of those who buy cheap and hope to sell at a higher price.

The concept may be confusing, but it's still quite simple. Your brokerage firm lends you a stock you agree to repurchase for a lower price. Several traders are masters in the use of this strategy. They must continually be glued to their screens to raise gains successfully. They primarily attack stocks that have increased excessively and which, sooner or later, will break from the pressure.

CHAPTER 4 – TREND INDICATORS

Various indicators remain at our disposal to analyze the chart of a stock. The indicators are primarily mathematical models based on two variables: stock price and periods. Each indicator has its strength. Use indicators as a complement to support, resistance and trend line. Let's start with the group of indicators used to follow trends: Simple Moving Average (SMA), Exponential Moving Average (EMA), Moving Average Convergence Divergence (MACD), Average Directional Index (ADX) and Parabolic SAR.

The trend indicators, as suggested by their names, allow you to highlight the trend of the market and stocks. The trend indicators are useful in sustaining the momentum indicators that we will see in **Chapter 5**. They have the advantage of giving a proven indication of the trend and the strength of this trend. The trends evolve cyclically, following an up-and-down sequence.

Trend indicators do not predict the future. No indicator can predict the future with accuracy. Still, it is reassuring to rely on such indicators when it is time to invest or sell. Furthermore, these indicators add weight to the trend line or channel you have drawn. The combination of several indicators will be more than positive and should improve your decisions before buying, selling or keeping a stock you already own.

Simple Moving Average (SMA)

The simple moving average represents the average price of a share over a given period. It's called moving because it moves from one period to another. Figure 4.1 presents, through a small circle, the moving average for the last 20 days (from August 12 to September 23). The gray zones form two independent groups of 20 days. A new moving average is calculated for each 20-day period.

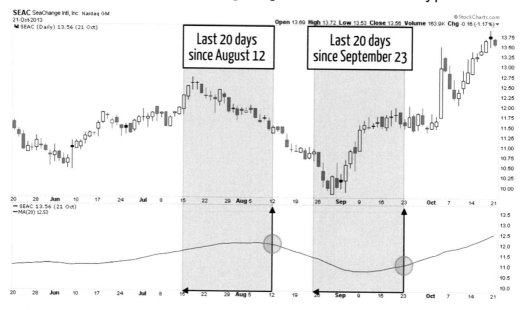

Figure 4.1 SEAC and SMA. Chart courtesy of StockCharts.com

The SMA is calculated starting from the number of periods (minutes, hours, days, weeks, weeks or months) listed in the settings of your provider. The calculation is very simple: it adds the closing price of the last 20 days, then divides by 20. To calculate the average of the following day, just remove the old date and add the most recent day. The juxtaposition of each day's average generates a smooth curve. The SMA also allows viewing the trend of the stock and identifying the change of the trend.

The shorter the moving average is, the more the moving average sticks to the trend. The more you increase the number of periods of the moving average, the more the gap between the average and the stock price will increase. The most popular averages are of 9, 13, 20, 30, 40, 50, 100, 150 and 200 periods. The crowd typically sticks with averages of 50 and 200 periods. Use the average that connects the best with your trading style. If you invest short-term, use the 30-day or 50-day moving average; if you invest long-term, use the 150-day or 200-day moving average.

Figure 4.2 Yahoo and SMA. Chart courtesy of StockCharts.com

It may seem that the price of a share tends to bounce on a moving average. It's not quite so. In fact, many investors check the same moving average, which makes the stock react at the same time. No matter the moving average used, you should buy a stock only when the slope of the moving average is rising. Figure 4.2 illustrates the rise of Yahoo stock during the first six months of the year 2013. Strangely, the SMA30 looks like a trend line.

The moving average, like all indicators, has a very nasty fault: It is a delayed indicator. It is late compared to the stock price. The moving average is not up to date; it is disconnected from the reality of the day. In a market that moves fast, the use of the moving average will be inefficient, unless you have your eyes continuously connected to your screen.

If you glue a short period to a moving average, such as five-day moving average, it will follow the rhythm of the share very tightly. Short moving averages are used by day traders. They use the crossing of the moving average and the share price as a point of entry or exit. A high moving average, such as a 200-day moving average, will be less sensitive to the variations of the stock price. It is recommended for long-term investors who do not worry much about short-term fluctuations.

Figure 4.3 Kandi Technologies & SMA 200 lagging. Chart courtesy of StockCharts.com

The above figure shows the impact generated by the 100% increase of Kandi Technologies on its 200-day moving average. The stock doubles in less than one week but has a slight impact on its moving average. As its name indicates, it is an average of the last 200 days. The delay between the SMA200 that points to $4 in early June 2013 and the stock price at $8 forces you to reevaluate the use of such an average. For this reason, favor the use of two moving averages.

The Strategy of Crossing Moving Averages

The decision to buy or sell may be made by using the intersection of two moving averages. This method consists of the use of two different moving averages, one for the short term and the other for the long term. The crossing generated through the use of these averages is a buy or sell signal.

It is suggested that you buy when the short-term moving average crosses above the longest average. It is also advised that you sell when the short-term moving average crosses below the longer average. Use a combination of 13-30 or 20-40 to generate a short-term signal. For a medium term, use a combination of 20-40 or 30-50, and for a long term use a 50-200 combination.

There are an infinite number of combinations. You can combine three moving averages as 13-21-34. Some people prove their originality and even use the Fibonacci sequence, which was introduced by

Leonard de Pise, surnamed Fibonacci. He was a mathematician of Italian origin who lived in the thirteenth century. The Fibonacci sequence is seen as the fact that each number, starting from the third one, is the sum of the two preceding numbers.

Here is the beginning of the Fibonacci sequence.

$$1, 1, 2, 3, 5, 8, 13, 21, 34, 55, 89, 144, 233...$$

The idea of using some of these numbers is not so farfetched. Pay attention to the Fibonacci sequence and see that the numbers 13, 21 and 34 are numbers that often reappear in the use of moving averages and other indicators. Feel free to create and test your combination! A combination can be efficient for one stock and inefficient for another one. In **Chapter 11**, we'll use another concept of Fibonacci.

In figure 4.4, an upward increase occurs in the second week of October 2012. The market will be positive for the next eight months. A big support is drawn at $32 after a few months (dotted horizontal line). The stock reaches a $35 limit in December 2012, makes a drop on the support zone and explodes at the beginning of 2013. While a stock unleashes a positive trend reversal, it is wise to tie the moving average to the subsequent return. The SMA13 serves as a support and trend line for the next months. A week closing below this average will send a sell signal.

Figure 4.4 Cree and buy signal. Chart courtesy of StockCharts.com

The combination of averages is a simple way to get buy and sell signals, but it also brings false signals. Avoid the signals generated during the consolidation period.

Exponential Moving Average (EMA)

An exponential moving average gives more weight to the most recent price instead of allocating the same weight every day as the simple moving average does. The exponential moving average is more spirited and responds faster to market volatility. Use a combination between the EMA 13-30 or EMA 13-34 on a weekly basis and pinpoint the cross for a reversal signal. These combinations are popular among the chartists.

Figure 4.5 Cree and EMA 13-30. Chart courtesy of StockCharts.com

You will notice that the EMA 13-SMA 30 combination of figure 4.5 is less sinuous than the SMA 13-30 combination of figure 4.4. The buy signal appears almost at the same time.

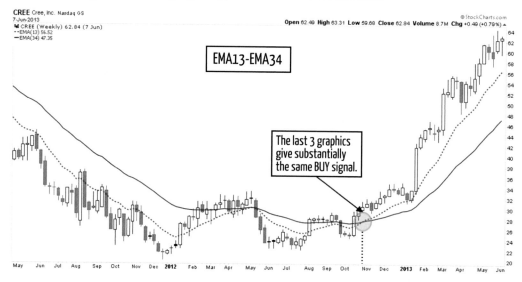

Figure 4.6 Cree and SMA13 EMA34. Chart courtesy of StockCharts.com

It is also possible to combine one EMA and one SMA to obtain both sides of the medal. For example, combine SMA13 and EMA34. Differences are more perceptible during ups and downs. During the period of consolidation, there is very little contrast.

> TACTICS - Moving Averages: A strategy based on crossing moving averages is much more efficient than using a single moving average. A bullish cross is generated when the shorter moving average crosses above the longer moving average. This often coincides with the start of Stage 2. Make sure you have a positive slope. A bearish cross is generated when the shortest moving average crosses below the longest average. The slope of the moving average should be negative.

Moving Average Convergence Divergence (MACD)

The MACD is a superb trend indicator. It is surely one of the most favorite indicators of many expert traders. This indicator is composed of three exponential moving averages (by default 12, 26, 9), and it is represented by two exponential curves, one slow and one fast. The crossing of the two curves gives a trading signal. The signal is bullish when the fast MACD passes above the slow MACD. The signal is bearish when the fast MACD passes below the slow MACD.

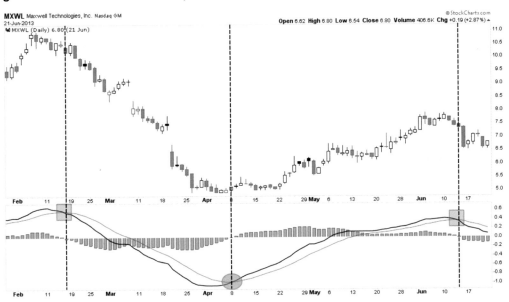

Figure 4.7 Maxwell Technologies and MACD. Chart courtesy of StockCharts.com

The above example shows the Maxwell Technologies stock with three superb MACD crossovers: one buy signal and two sell signals. MACD crossing indicates a change in the market trend. Notice how the signals have very little delay compared to the stock price.

The farther the signal is away from zero, the more pertinent the signal will be. Furthermore, notice the beautiful amplitude of the indicator. These signals are reliable and indicate more precisely the direction the market will take. Favor stocks that offer this kind of amplitude – the suggested trend will be even more precise.

The MACD histogram is shown in the background as the vertical blue bars. The histogram represents the difference between the two curves of MACD and indicates a buy or sell signal when the MACD crossing is made. When the MACD indicator gives a buy signal, the histogram is above the zero line. The buyers took control. When the MACD indicator launches a sell signal, the histogram is below the zero line.

The slope of the histogram begins to turn upward March 27. This signal appeared five days before the signal from the MACD lines. Above all, don't forget the MACD histogram, as it is particularly efficient.

The MACD indicator is also useful for detecting divergences. Remember that a divergence appears when the indicator goes against the stock price, and it allows identifying possible reversals. But these could be fake signals. Be very careful with these divergences.

Figure 4.8 AAPL and MACD divergence. Chart courtesy of StockCharts.com

Apple shows, in the figure above, a huge negative divergence in March 2012. This divergence is extended to the six-month period. During this period, the investors who took advantage of the rise still obtained a 20% gain. They should be more cautious when the MACD indicator crosses downward in October 2012.

Average Directional Index (ADX)

The average directional index (ADX) is a trend indicator, as well as a trend strength indicator. This is a trading system on its own, because it allows you to generate several signals. It is represented through three curves: +DI, -DI and ADX. The +DI measures the bullish pressure while the -DI measures the bearish pressure. The ADX curve measures the force related to this upward or downward pressure.

It's important to remember that the ADX curve does not follow the trend of the market. It goes more in the direction of the market strength, upward as well as downward. This last concept is a little more difficult to understand.

It is common to go long when the +DI curve passes above the -DI curve. Your position will strengthen when the ADX indicator is in an uptrend. The +DI and -DI curves are the following trend indicators of this system. When the ADX is higher than 20 and the +DI curve passes above the -DI curve, a buy signal is generated. The ADX must be used on a weekly chart. When the ADX is higher than 20 and the -DI curve passes above the +DI curve, a sell signal is registered.

It is important to consider not only the crossing of +DI and -DI as a buy signal. A buy signal is in place when a trend reversal of the +DI and -DI curves appears. Instead of waiting for the +DI to cross above the -DI, think about investing when the +DI comes out of a major low.

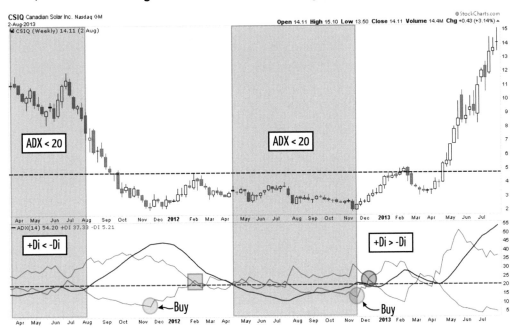

Figure 4.9 Canadian Solar and ADX. Chart courtesy of StockCharts.com

The indicators have to be used carefully. Let's take a look at the Canadian Solar stock just above. See the time elapsed between the first buy signal by the +DI (black arrow on the left) and the blue circle.

The +DI and −DI crosses appeared almost three months after the significant depression made by the +DI. Substantial gains have been simply put aside. Furthermore, notice that this first crossing between the +DI and −DI appeared late, because it occurred at the same time as the stock began a decline of about ten weeks.

Strong buy signals appear when the ADX (black line) is placed significantly below the 20 line, makes a return and the +DI crosses above the −DI as represented by the green circles. Complete this with a big volume and you'll have an exponential rise.

The ADX measures the power of the trend. The higher it is, the stronger the trend. Pay attention to the first climb that reaches level 45. A strong downward movement is established. CSIQ lost 80% of its value in five months. Investors sold out their shares massively, which led to a faster drop of the stock. On the other side, we can see the same phenomenon but opposite. The stock has grown from $3 to $12 in less than three months. The rise, extremely powerful, was confirmed by a quick surge of the ADX.

> TACTICS − ADX. The positive trend is confirmed when the +DI crosses the −DI and ADX exceed 20. Consider investing when the +DI begins to form a significant depression. The decline of the ADX signals the consolidation or the indecision of the market. Avoid transactions during this period. The ADX indicates the power of the trend. It is important to understand that the ADX may be high during a bullish or bearish market. When the ADX falls below 10, the trend does not practically exist. Be prepared to identify any bullish movement.

Parabolic SAR

The Parabolic SAR, where SAR means "stop and reversal," is an indicator created by J. Welles Wilder. This indicator informs about potential trend changes in stock price or stock market index. It clearly shows the beginning and the end of a trend.

Parabolic SAR is represented through simple squares placed above and below the candlesticks. A square below the candlestick indicates that the trend is upward. A square above the candlestick indicates that the trend is downward. Pay attention to the trend changes; the square changes place. The signal is simple, but useful.

The calculation for setting up the resultant curve of the Parabolic SAR is very complicated. We would rather explain its use. To understand better, pay attention to the chart of Advanced Micro Devices from figure 4.10. The small squares over and under the stock price represent the trend and are grouped by sequences.

We have added little shapes that show the triggering component (yellow circle), the start of a bullish trend (green circle) and the beginning of a bearish trend (red square). The trigger is the candlestick that blocks the way of a brand new square and forces the present trend to end.

When the catalyst component (yellow) stumbles on a candlestick, a stop is automatically triggered to put an end to the trend in order to start a fresh one. It can be an upward trend, identified by a green circle, or a downward trend, identified by a red square. It is an excellent system for traders who sell their bad position late and who are stubborn to keep it. Evaluate the effectiveness of the system on your own. The bullish and bearish signals conform quite closely to the cycle of the share.

Figure 4.10 Advanced Micro Devices and SAR. Chart courtesy of StockCharts.com

Notice the small blue circle that highlights a square, isolated between two downtrends. That is unusual in a weekly chart. A stock market is composed of bull and bear cycles. These cycles usually have a minimal duration of three or four weeks. In the case of consolidation market, which moves sideways or in an unstable market, this indicator could transmit many false signals. This is why you should always support your decisions through other indicators.

> TACTICS – Parabolic SAR: It is recommended that you use the indicator for a weekly period, unless the market shows an absence of volatility. Combine this indicator with another trend indicator such as MACD or ADX.

CHAPTER 5 – MOMENTUM INDICATORS

Momentum indicators, or oscillators, represent indicators of reversal that expect a change in a relatively short space of time. These indicators respond quickly to different signals emitted by the stock and can highlight some dissonances or divergences. Your trading system must include at least one oscillator.

Working with oscillators only requires you to do day trading because these indicators react quickly to the movements of the market. Nowadays, the most popular oscillators are the Stochastic, the Relative Strength Index (RSI) and the Rate of Change (ROC).

Stochastic

The Stochastic indicator was popularized in the late 1950s by Georges Lane. It is an oscillator that reacts rapidly, even before the stock price. There are several types of Stochastic, and we pay attention to the slow Stochastic, which offers fewer distortions than the fast Stochastic. The Stochastic tends to predict the turning points comparing the closing price of a stock to its price range, between the highest and the lowest level.

This indicator is presented on a scale from 0 to 100. Two horizontal lines that serve as a threshold are shown in the background. The lower threshold is 20, and the upper threshold is 80. Most of the tools for chartists fix the average of 14 days. Two important rules result from this.

The first rule: when the Stochastic passes below 20, the stock is oversold. It simply means that the stock price is too low compared to its historical price from the last 14 days. The immediate consequence should be to buy, but it is not so simple. The Stochastic shows that the stock is oversold and has some potential to purchase, nothing more. This is an extremist indicator which acts quickly. It is a signal that incites investors to prepare for action.

The second rule: when the Stochastic passes above 80, the stock is overbought. It simply means that the stock price is excessively high compared to its historical price from the last 14 days. The immediate consequence should be to liquidate, nothing more. Be prepared to act. Stochastic shows a stock that is potentially too expensive.

The Stochastic is made of two curves: a fast and a slow curve. It's the same principle as the MACD: the signal is bullish when the fast Stochastic passes above the slow. The signal is bearish when the fast Stochastic falls below the slow.

This simply means that the stock is low compared to its recent historical price; nothing proves that it could not fall anymore. We could even say that we buy a dropping value. It is better to wait patiently until the value stabilizes a bit and thinks about changing direction. It's preferable to buy when the Stochastic passes over 20.

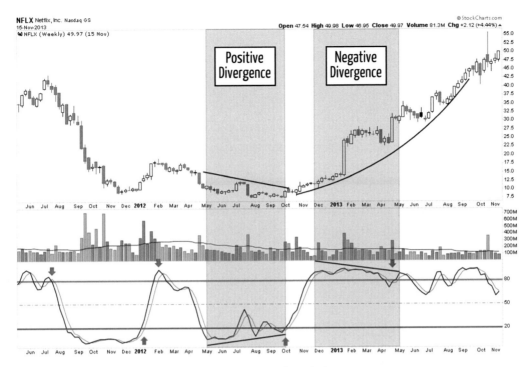

Figure 5.1 Netflix and Stochastic. Chart courtesy of StockCharts.com

Look at the weekly chart of Netflix. There is much analysis to do for this chart. First of all, take a look at the arrows that present the direction changes triggered by the crossing of the slow and fast Stochastic. The first three arrows gave excellent signals. Then, pay attention to the first gray zone. A positive divergence is drawn to give a more powerful rally, making the stock go from $75 to $250 in seven months. The Stochastic has simply refused to reach a lower level and has crossed 20 to launch an upward signal.

The second gray zone presents a negative divergence spread over six months. Throughout this period, the stock has not ceased to climb. To establish a trend, a parabolic line has been drawn under the stock price. It allows establishing an exit point at $225 while the crossing of the Stochastic indicates a possible exit was set at $250. After analysis, we agree that this divergence sends a false signal. You should always use another indicator or a trend line to support your action.

TACTICS – Stochastic: A stock that is overbought has strong chances of declining. A stock that is oversold is likely to rise. The divergences between the Stochastic lines and the stock price represent a potential signal of change in the trend. During an uptrend, the Stochastic tends to remain in an overbought situation, which is not necessarily a sell signal. In a downtrend, the Stochastic tends to remain in an oversold situation, which does not represent a buy signal. Favor the stocks with an upward trend when the Stochastic has come with an oversold level. It could be quite possible that the stock will make a slight drop before continuing to rise.

Relative Strength Index (RSI)

The Relative Strength Indicator (RSI) is an oscillator that measures the internal strength of a stock that sails between the threshold of 0 and 100. The upper zone, between 70 and 100, is an overbought zone and the lower zone, between 0 and 30, is an oversold zone. It means that you should act in these two zones. The 30-70 level is just a transition between the two main areas.

By default, the number of periods is set at 14, but you can use other periods such as 5, 7, 9, 11 or 13. The situations when we use a period higher than 14 are unusual, because the curve will be too smooth and respond to the price amplitudes slower. RSI is useful for identifying some divergences needed to anticipate the trends of different stocks or major indexes.

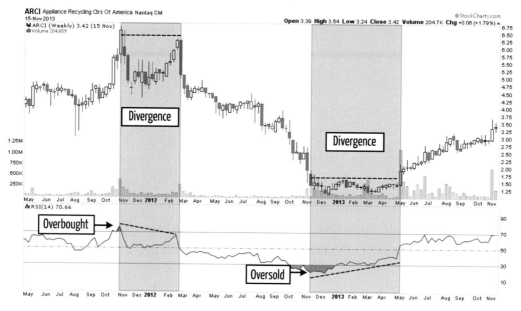

Figure 5.2 Appliance Recycling and RSI. Chart courtesy of StockCharts.com

Look at the relationship between the RSI and the stock price of Appliance Recycling. When the RSI is higher than 70 (overbought) or lower than 30 (oversold), it launches a potential reversal signal. This chart also shows two divergences between the RSI and the stock price. The first divergence is negative. RSI has been unable to make a new high. The second divergence is positive. RSI goes higher when the stock makes no progress. These divergences have been highly effective. Pay attention to the divergences that are being prepared in the overbought or oversold zones, as these are the most important to watch.

TACTICS – RSI: Set the bar higher for overbought and oversold situations. Use the target of 20-25 for the oversold and the target of 80-85 for the overbought. The indicator is useful in spotting the divergences that may announce changes in the trends for stock price or index. Pay less attention to the divergences within the 30-70 range.

Rate of Change (ROC)

The ROC is a momentum oscillator which allows measuring the progression speed of a stock. Its curve looks similar to the one of RSI, but axes are different. Two zones are present: a negative one and a positive one. The middle zone of the indicator is represented through zero while the central level for the RSI is represented by the number 50. There is no upward or downward boundary.

ROC compares the closing price of the period with the one of another period (usually 12). ROC on the rise shows that the progression of the stock has been greater than the reference period. The share is overbought, and the upward trend is likely to continue. On the other hand, when the ROC is low, the stock is considered oversold and the downward trend is expected to continue. The stock price tends to climb when the ROC is greater than zero. The share price tends to go down when the ROC is below zero.

A stock that goes up while the ROC decreases indicates a top is near. A stock that goes down while the ROC increases indicate that a new low is very close. Some providers of stock charts have an ROC histogram instead of a curve. In addition, note that the scale of values of the ROC is different for every stock, which might be a little confusing.

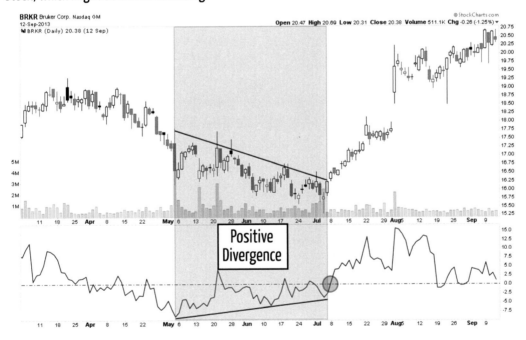

Figure 5.3 Bruker Corp and daily ROC. Chart courtesy of StockCharts.com

Use this indicator to locate the divergences that may affect the stock trend. As for the RSI, the more the divergences are distanced from the central area, the more weight they will have. Figure 5.3 illustrates the divergence between the ROC and the stock price of Bruker Corp. In early May, the ROC registered a low and continued its climb while the stock was falling. This situation indicates that a reversal is about to happen.

At the beginning of July, the stock reached its lowest level of the last four months. Notice the volume associated with this bottom. There was panic among the sellers, and the buyers took advantage of this chance to buy cheap.

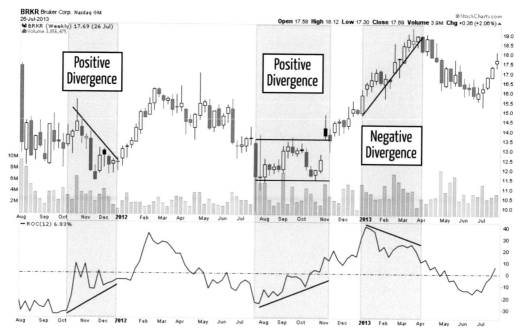

Figure 5.4 Bruker Corp and weekly ROC. Chart courtesy of StockCharts.com

Figure 5.4 illustrates the weekly chart of Bruker Corp. Notice the divergences announcing the trend reversals. In addition, pay attention to the vertical scale of the ROC, which is quite different from that of the daily chart shown in figure 5.3. This representation requires us to invent landmarks for every stock because the scale is not static like in RSI or Stochastic.

> TACTICS – ROC: The more the indicator rises above the equilibrium level, the more the stock is overbought. The more the stock falls below the equilibrium level, the more the stock is oversold. This indicator is useful for locating the divergences that may set changes in trends of a stock or index. The RSI indicator presents a better alternative, because the axes have the same threshold for all the stocks.

Chaikin Money Flow

The Chaikin Money Flow has been developed by Marc Chaikin. This indicator is different from other momentum indicators by the fact that combines the price and volume, while most indicators of momentum base their calculations only on price.

It is an indicator of an indicator because it bases its calculations on the Accumulation/Distribution indicator. It makes two comparisons. Firstly, it compares the closing price with the high/low range. Secondly, it compares the result obtained with total volume for the same interval.

When the Chaikin Money Flow is above zero, it indicates that we are in a period of accumulation. When the Chaikin Money Flow is less than zero, this indicates that we are in a period of distribution. The farther the indicator is from zero, the more important the strength of the signal.

It allows you to highlight pressure on a buyer or seller related to a share. This indicator will be positive when prices regularly close near their top. The result is a signal of strength. It will be negative if the stock price regularly closes at the lowest level. This is a weak signal.

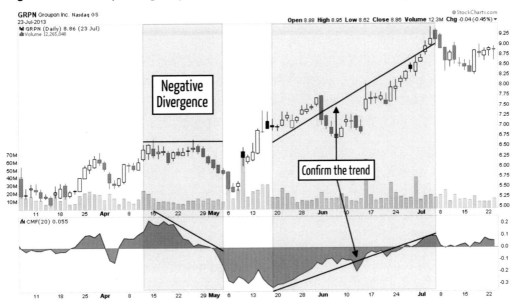

Figure 5.5 Groupon and Chaikin Money Flow. Chart courtesy of StockCharts.com

Look at the daily chart of Groupon. First of all, there is a negative divergence well announced by the Chaikin Money Flow. Secondly, note the support given to the stock price through the indicator. Since the stock always closes near the previous close, this accentuates the pressure on the buyer and involves an increase of the Chaikin Money Flow. In early July, buying pressure is reduced, and it brings the Chaikin Money Flow back in a good, balanced position.

> TACTICS – Chaikin Money Flow: The Chaikin Money Flow is an interesting way to detect accumulation and distribution phases. Divergences between the indicator and prices can also provide valuable insights on their own about the evolution of the trend that begins to take shape.

CHAPTER 6 – VOLATILITY INDICATORS

The volatility indicators reflect the change in stock price. The wider the stock gaps, the more powerful the volatility index will be. Volatility increases when the stock price fluctuates in a wider range of value. A share with modest volatility announces the weak amplitude of the stock price. The volatility of a stock has nothing to do with the trend, but rather with the amplitude of the upward or downward movement.

Bollinger Bands

This trend indicator appears in the form of an envelope whose middle is a 20-period SMA. The bands correspond to an upper and lower margin based on the SMA. The spacing of the bands shows the volatility level in a stock or an indicator. The more bands are discarded, the more volatility is present. When the share price exceeds the envelope, this indicates a potential turnaround.

Some financial strategists recommend monitoring all exits of the lower band and taking action the next day when it is obvious that the stock will close higher than the day before. There is no way to know if the selling pressure will continue after this rebound. Let's look at the example below. The eBay stock generated ten exits of the lower band during February and March before a major turnaround, which began March 18.

Figure 6.1 EBay and Bollinger bands. Chart courtesy of StockCharts.com

To better ensure you're covered, invest when the stock passes over the dotted median line. As is shown in figure 6.1, eBay does not remain bullish for a long time, but it allows a small 5% return twice in April and May. Do not make any investment decision based simply on the fact that the share is outside the Bollinger bands.

The greatest strength of the Bollinger bands resides in their use on a weekly basis. Monitor securities whose envelope shrinks significantly. Taken alone, the contraction means lack of volatility. However, this indicates that a significant event will happen in the short or medium term, upward and downward, one that we are unable to predict for the moment.

Figure 6.2 SPWR Bollinger bands contraction. Chart courtesy of StockCharts.com

Watch the explosion generated in December 2012 by the contraction of the Bollinger bands on the SunPower stock from figure 6.2. The bands gradually contracted for 12 months before widening again. The stock exploded in December 2012 from $4 to $20 in less than seven months.

> TACTICS – Bollinger bands: Combined with other indicators, the Bollinger bands are an indicator of choice in your trading system. Consider investing only when the stock passes above the median band. Furthermore, go long when the median is upward. Monitor the contractions of the bands. They announce a change in trend that could be explosive.

Average True Range (ATR)

The average true range is an excellent indicator for measuring the volatility of a stock. This indicator does not detect the direction or the market trend. Rather, ATR is an unbounded indicator which allows measuring the investor interest in a stock or index. It measures the average between the highest and the lowest levels. A high ATR indicates steep volatility, and a low ATR indicates a soft volatility level.

When the indicator has little variation during a certain period, this suggests that the line is in a narrow trading range. Periods of low volatility announce violent movements in prices. When the ATR presents higher levels, up or down, it suggests a possible trend reversal. Draw trend lines to estimate an entry or exit point. This point of entry or exit may be the beginning of a new explosive trend.

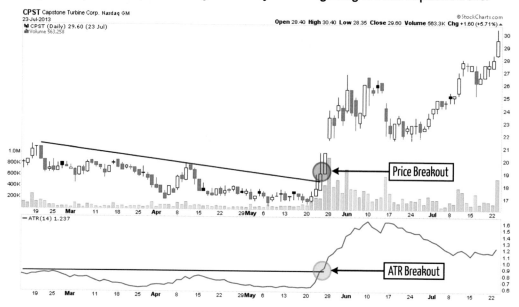

Figure 6.3 Capstone Turbide and ATR. Chart courtesy of StockCharts.com

The above figure highlights the relationship between the ATR and the stock price. During the ATR's trend breakout, there is an increase of 50% for Capstone Turbide. The period of low volatility from February to May 2013 prepared us for a possible change of direction of the share price.

TACTICS – Average True Range: Periods of low volatility precede bull and bear movements. The high interest of investors does not necessarily mean that the trend is about to reverse.

CHAPTER 7 – VOLUME INDICATORS

The main indicators are based on stock price and also on stock volume. Volume indicators are mainly used to confirm trends and to alert you to a possible trend reversal. The emotional implications of traders have to materialize through volumes. In this chapter, we will talk about the indicators that directly come from the volume and offer the possibility of increasing bullish or bearish signals. These indicators have been developed to help in decision-making and to furnish more explicit signals.

Volume

This indicator shows the number of transactions exchanged by period (minutes, hours, days, weeks, etc.). For many traders, the volume is the only indicator used to make a good buying decision. It is logical. Other technical indicators constantly use the volume in their formulas. The volume is the basis of technical analysis. An increase in the price of a share with big volumes indicates that this increase is approved by the markets. A decrease of stock price with high volumes indicates that the decrease is also confirmed by markets.

Figure 7.1 Intel Corp & Volume. Chart courtesy of StockCharts.com

The figure above provides much information through the volumes of Intel Corp. We have added a moving average to make a rapprochement with stages seen before. Each day has its volume bar, a gray bar for the days when the stock price is rising and a red bar for the days of decline. We have also drawn some trend lines. Here are seven important points connected to the volumes.

Point 1

The stock has just ended a consolidation period with a fairly stable volume level. It completes its Stage 1. The volume level is increasing. The stock comes out of the trend channel, and breaks its SMA30 and crossover trend channel.

Point 2

The stock is in Stage 2. The positive trend is supported by a significant increase in the volume of transactions. An uptrend must be supported by a strong volume. The volume drops rapidly during this stage, which could have damaged the duration of this upward movement.

Point 3

We are in Stage 3, which is the consolidation stage. The volume level is inferior, except for temporary revival. The stock registers an increase with the volume level lower than the one in Stage 2.

Point 4

Breaking Stage 3 and breaking the SMA30, Stage 4 is taking shape. Some buyers believe that the boost will continue and do not want to miss their chance to make fabulous profits.

Point 5

The stock collapses even more, but comes back to test the support area. There is a significant volume increase, which is not obligatory during a Stage 3 breakout. In a bearish panic situation, volumes can greatly increase.

Point 6

The buyers are testing the support zone. The volume peaks are irregular. Future losers have just entered the game.

Point 7

It comes to the final test of the resistance/support area. Sellers abdicate, the volume increases and Stage 4 continues.

Intraday Volume

Experience will allow you to observe that there are two moments in the day when the activity level is highest: opening and closing of the markets. Many traders put their energies in only at the beginning and at the end of a session, because it is precisely there that we find the greatest changes in the price of a stock. The midday portion usually offers less volatility and volume.

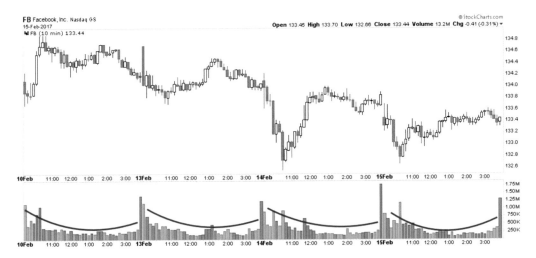

Figure 7.2 Facebook intraday Volume. Chart courtesy of StockCharts.com

Look at the above figure of Facebook and pay attention to the parabolic distribution of volume for a few days. The volume is higher in the beginning and at the end of a session than in the middle of the day. We see that the first half-hour provides the highest volume level of the day. Frequently, the stock price reached in the first half an hour could not be surpassed for the rest of the day. The volume decrease in the midday is caused by the market makers who step out of the office for lunch.

Volume by Price

This indicator shows the volume associated with different price levels. It is represented through the horizontal bars which act as support and resistance at distinct price levels. The bars are based on the required period. For example, for a five-year weekly chart, the bars represent the data during the five years. The longer the bar, the more significant the support/resistance level will be.

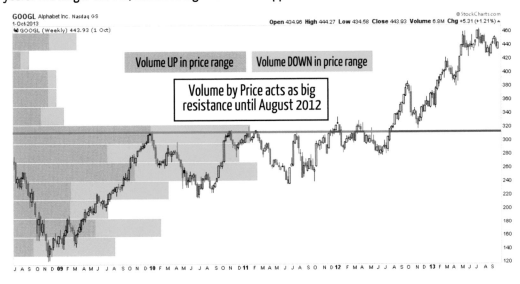

Figure 7.3 Google and volume by price. Chart courtesy of StockCharts.com

The above chart of Google shows that level of $320 was a resistance and became the support after August 2012. We can agree that, in the event of the fall of this stock, it could return to that $320 level, since this support had been raised for three years. The use of this indicator, among others, predicts the limits that the stock could bounce.

All data are taken into consideration for the required period. It's implied that the most important support level revealed for this five-year chart could be different for a chart covering the last six months. It is necessary to have a portrait of volume by price on a weekly and daily time frame

> TACTICS. Volume by price: Use the bars of the Volume by Price to anticipate areas of support and resistance on which stock price could bounce. Draw the most important support and resistance lines. Work on daily and weekly chart to determine key levels. Consider this indicator as a fundamental element of your technical analysis system.

Accumulation/Distribution

This indicator allows you to isolate phases of accumulation and distribution. It is a useful indicator for confirming current trends. When the indicator is placed in a positive trend, meaning higher highs and higher lows, the stock is in a period of accumulation. Conversely, the stock is in a distribution period when the Accumulation/Distribution curve is in a downtrend, which means lower highs and lower lows.

Use this indicator to confirm the trend of the share price. Equally, learn to spot the divergences between the Accumulation/Distribution curve and the stock price. The divergence sends a potential reversal signal. A divergence is bullish when prices are in a downward trend while the indicator is ascendant. A divergence is bearish when prices are in uptrend while the indicator is descendant.

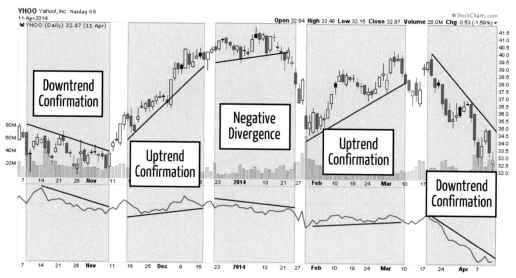

Figure 7.4 Yahoo and Accumulation/Distribution. Chart courtesy of StockCharts.com

The above chart presents four confirmations of a trend supported by the Accumulation/Distribution curve: two uptrends and two downtrends. These confirmations allow an investor to add weight to his decision of investing during the increase or of selling short while the stocks decline.

Pay particular attention to stocks that have a long accumulation period. There is a chance that a resistance break can generate a strong buy signal. These stocks have a huge potential, but the wait can be quite long. Your patience could be put through a tough test. Observe that the volume weight is more significant on the highest price of the shares than on the lowest price.

The central zone presents a divergence between the Accumulation/Distribution and the share price. The stock is unable to close higher than its resistance line while the Accumulation/Distribution drops during four weeks. This divergence announces the probable appearance – or the possibility – of coming decline. That is precisely what happened in late December 2013.

> TACTICS – Accumulation/Distribution: The indicator can be used to confirm an uptrend or a downtrend. It is useful in spotting divergences that may announce changes in trend in stock price or index.

On Balance Volume (OBV)

On balance volume, or OBV, is an indicator with no threshold, which means that it does not have any scales. The OBV is a net volume accumulator. When the price closes above the preceding closing price, volume is added to the OBV of the day. When the price closes below the previous closing price, we subtract the volume from the OBV of the day.

This indicator allows you to isolate phases of accumulation and distribution. It is a useful indicator for highlighting divergences and confirming current trends. The OBV confirms a positive trend when the ups and downs are often higher. The OBV confirms a downward trend when the highs and lows are much lower.

The OBV indicator compares the entries and the exits of a stock with its volume. The steady increase in stock price should normally be supported at least by a constant volume. Without this support of volumes, the stock price will eventually fall. Beyond the divergence detection, the OBV allows determining the entry points during the trend reversal.

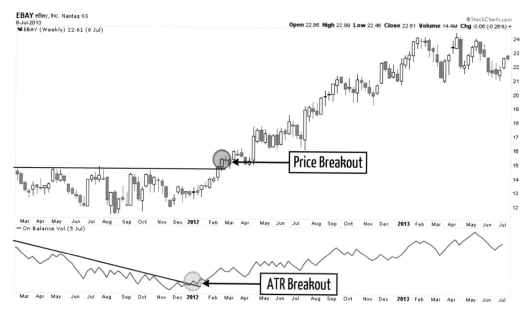

Figure 7.5 EBay On balance volume. Chart courtesy of StockCharts.com

The downward trend break of the OBV indicates that you should buy Ebay in early 2012 even before the stock started his extraordinary rise. See how the OBV has supported the rising of the share for 18 months.

> TACTICS – On balance volume: OBV indicator serves to confirm an uptrend or a downtrend. The indicator is useful in spotting the divergences that may announce trend changes in stock or index. Pull trend lines and pay attention to the breaking targets. They can announce beautiful reversals.

Force Index

The force index is an oscillator that measures the strength of bullish and bearish movements. The indicator is an unbounded indicator. The force index represents the multiplication of the volume of the day by the difference between the closing price of the day and the closing price of the previous day. This calculation allows you to highlight the trend as well as the strength of the trend.

The indicator comes in the form of peaks with a central line of zero. An indicator below zero means a negative force. The bears are in control. An indicator above zero reveals a positive force. The bulls are in control. The particularity of this indicator is that it can be used in the short, medium and long term. You could use it with different averages to highlight the divergences and trends that may be drawn. We greatly favor the use of 2-day and 13-day periods.

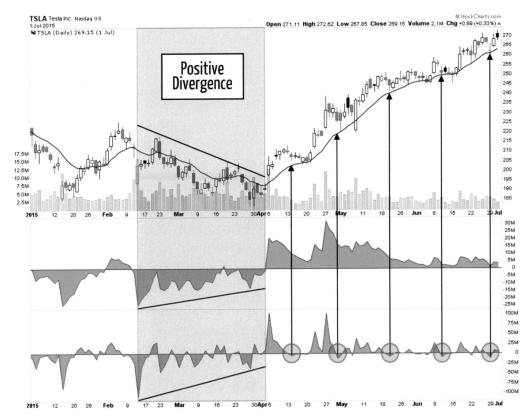

Figure 7.6 Tesla & force index. Chart courtesy of StockCharts.com

The above figure shows Tesla stock and two force indicators, a 2-day and a 13-day. Indicators significantly send the same signals except that they are more visible when set at two periods. The 13-day force index is smoother than the 2-day.

Consider these basic rules when negotiating stocks based on the force index. Buy when the 2-day force index becomes negative during a positive trend. Make a short sale when the 2-day becomes positive in a downward market. Consider the divergences. Buy when the prices decrease to a lower level while the force index reaches a higher low.

CHAPTER 8 – CONTINUATION PATTERNS

Continuation patterns refer to configurations that mark a pause during a trend. These breaks are consolidation periods which will allow the stock to continue its trend with the same vigor and often in a more explosive way. These patterns are numerous and can be recognized by many traders and even by software or trading tools.

Cup and Handle

The Cup and Handle was discovered and put forward by William J. O'Neil in his book How to Make Money in Stocks. The Cup and Handle is usually the continuation of a bullish trend. This pattern is made of two rounded bottoms. The first bottom, deeper, represents the Cup, while the second bottom represents the Handle.

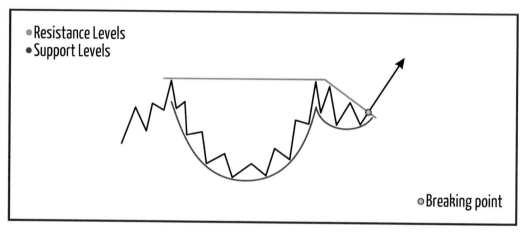

Figure 8.1 The Cup and Handle pattern is a particular figure found quite frequently in different stock markets. It remains very efficient on breakout with large volumes. After spotting a stock with this kind of configuration on a weekly chart, place it on a watchlist. It is likely to generate significant gains.

The primary bottom draws the neckline and the resistance threshold. The second bottom, smaller and more concentrated, ends with a breakout coupled with a relevant increase in the volume. As in any breakout, the volume stays the most significant factor to monitor. Without any volume increase, the break of the resistance line is almost impossible.

The figure 8.2 shows the Cup and Handle generated by Noah Holdings. The pattern extends on over 14 months. It adds even more weight to the breakout that occurred in May 2013. A neckline at $8.25 appears in October 2011. The first bottom extends over a period of 12 months. During this period, no attempt to test resistance was made. In March 2013, a pullback was performed under the neckline to draw the second bottom, a smaller one. The objective from the neckline is equivalent to the height of the first bottom.

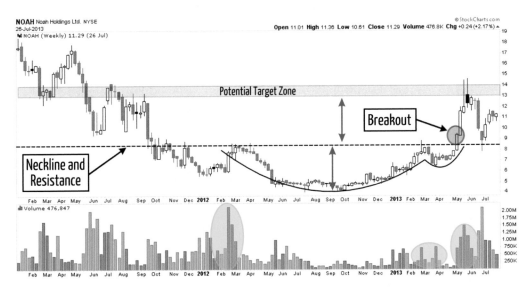

Figure 8.2 Noah Holdings & Cup and handle. Chart courtesy of StockCharts.com

Cup and Handle is one of the most winning figures, with a success rate between 70% and 80%. Give priority to the signals generated on a weekly chart. When you have the chance to detect one, monitor it closely, because it offers significant potential gains.

Dead-Cat Bounce

The term "dead-cat bounce" comes from the idea that even when dead, a cat will bounce back if it falls. The rebound will be not as high as if the cat had been living, though. The same thing happens in the stock market. A share that suffers from a decline will finish, sooner or later, by a reversal to the upside.

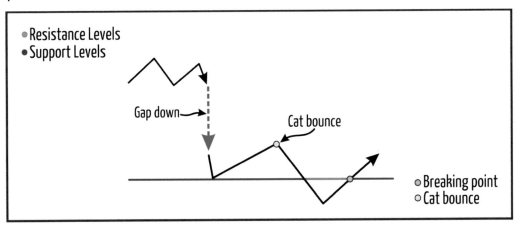

Figure 8.3 The dead-cat bounce pattern is a passive model. It refers to a past event where the premises cannot be predicted. The sharp drop at the market opening is often due to bad economic news related to the stock or markets. It may take up to 12 months to close the gap generated at the beginning of the fall.

Quite often, this configuration begins with a huge downward gap which follows the publication of bad economic news. A fast bounce-back of a stock is rare. This configuration is a trend continuation pattern. The downward trend should follow a light bounce-back. The highest impulse represents the "cat bounce."

This reversal of the situation could be temporary. The period of consolidation typically ranges from two to 12 months. At best, you can expect to earn from 10% to 15% on the rebound. Place this stock on your watchlist. The breakout of the resistance line will be your first buy signal.

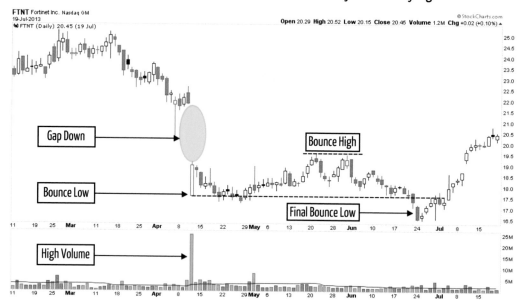

Figure 8.4 Fortinet and dead cat bounce. Chart courtesy of StockCharts.com

The above chart of Fortinet Company shows a 30% drop of the stock from its summit in March 2013. The share price stabilizes and rebounds by 10%. It is the dead-cat bounce. Consequently, the stock comes back to the bounce zone and breaks this support zone later. This last capitulation offers munitions, and the stock goes up rapidly, as the pros smelled a good opportunity. There are chances to close the initial gap on this climb.

Triangle – Ascending Triangle

The ascending triangle is a continuation pattern with an upward trend. It is the most popular pattern among traders, as well as one of the most present on the stock market. This pattern represents an intermediate phase, a pause in a rising trend. The ascending triangle is represented through a horizontal line – the resistance over which the stock price stumbles – and by a diagonal, which offers support.

As time passes, the stock price rises back towards the resistance level and it breaks it with high volumes. Even though it is very popular, this pattern still sends many false signals that cause significant losses to investors.

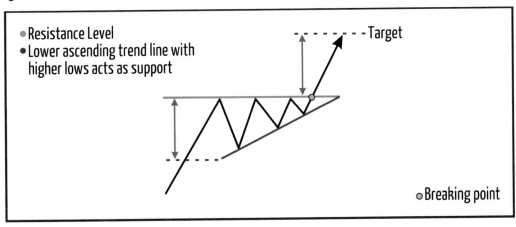

Figure 8.5 The ascending triangle is a pattern very valued by small and large investors. For beginners, it is easy to spot on daily and weekly chart. The breaking volume is essential. Closely monitor the stocks that have tested the resistance line several times before. The break could generate big profits.

We can never repeat enough that it is essential to have a high volume on the resistance break. This volume must be three to five times HIGHER than the average volume of the last 30 periods. Without this condition, you expose yourself to a potential quick reversal which may lead to significant losses.

Two groups are opposed when handling this model. The pros sell when the stock reaches its resistance, and others buy hoping for an upward break of the prices. Pros could sell everything just above the break, when they realize that the volume does not meet anticipations. They take advantage of this false signal to short sale, suspecting that the stock will return downwards.

The potential target is equivalent to the height of the triangle added to the resistance level. This target remains approximate. A triangle with a minimum of 20 periods is required to generate a good breakout. To be valid, the two lines forming the triangle must be touched three times by the candlesticks.

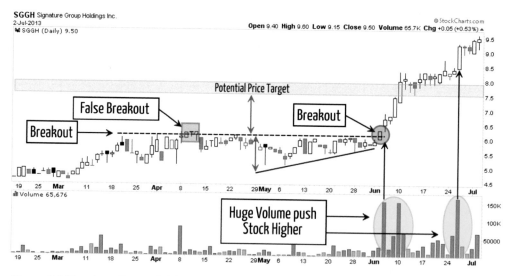

Figure 8.6 Signature Group Holdings and ascending triangle. Chart courtesy of StockCharts.com

Pay attention to the figure above and look at the number of times that the share price of Signature Group Holdings tests the resistance line representing the top of the triangle. The tests prior to the formation of the triangle would have shaped an extremely powerful breakout. Now, pay attention to the false breakout signal identified by a blue square. First, the break is not sufficient to confirm the breakout. Furthermore, no volume increase has come to sustain this resistance break.

Several experts suggest that the breakout should be at 2/3 of the triangle, before the two lines of the triangle would touch each other. A break at 2/3 would indicate that the buyers had won the fight and were hastening to continue. Figures 8.6 and 8.7 tend to confirm this theory. However, the most important element remains the volume power.

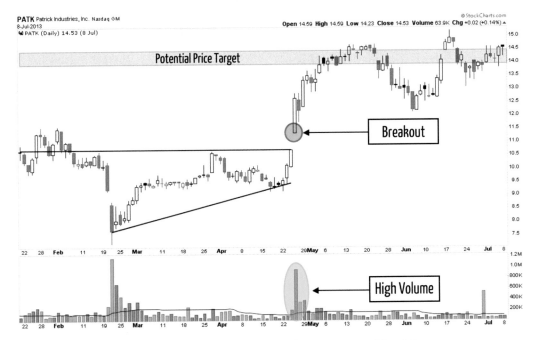

Figure 8.7 Patrick Industries & ascending triangle. Chart courtesy of StockCharts.com

A chart of Patrick Industries shows an upward triangle built in an irregular way extended over 40 days. The stock price tested the resistance twice at halfway. In late May 2013, the volume strength of the breakout is unequivocal.

We assist to a strong break, built in a period of more than two months. The volume is equivalent to at least ten times the average volume of the previous 30 days. During such an increase, it is quite natural to observe the appearance of a gap. This gap launches a signal to the markets that the stock is undervalued, draining many investors to new highs.

Triangle – Descending Triangle

Opposite to the ascending triangle, the descending triangle is a bearish continuation pattern. It stands for an intermediary phase, a pause in a downward trend. The descending triangle is formed by a horizontal line that represents the support on which the stock price rests, as well as a diagonal representing the declining resistance.

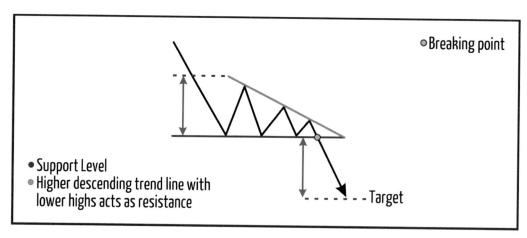

Figure 8.8 Descending triangle pattern. This model is very effective. If you are invested, think about selling your stock, because the fall is predictable.

Two groups are opposed: the pros sell when the stock reaches its resistance and the others buy, hoping for an upward break of the prices. As time passes by, the stock price decreases and just breaks the support level. It's not required to have an increase in volume during the breakdown. The potential target is equivalent to the height of the triangle, subtracted from the support line. This target remains approximate.

Figure 8.9 Silver & descending triangle. Chart courtesy of StockCharts.com

The figure above illustrates a beautiful descending triangle for silver. The descending triangle extends over two years. To be valid, the two lines that shape the triangle should be touched at least three times by the candlesticks.

We can consider a possible target of $7.5 for the stock price ($27.5-[$47.5-$27.5]). Think about a support area between $17.50 and $20. The target of $7.5 remains highly exaggerated. Notice the slight increase during the break of the $27.5 support zone.

As any breakout, the downward break of the triangle should appear at 2/3 of the triangle, which means before the two lines of the triangle touch each other. A break at 2/3 would indicate that the sellers had won the battle and were eager to continue the fight. Volume on breakdown has much less importance than a break to the upside.

Flag and Pennant Bull Pattern

The flag and the pennant are patterns found at rallies supported by the strong fundamental news. The flag and the pennant are favourable breaks in the pursuit of a stock's upward trend. This pause is beneficial and creates a comfort zone. The transition period is marked by a lower volume just before the stock begins to fly on strong volume.

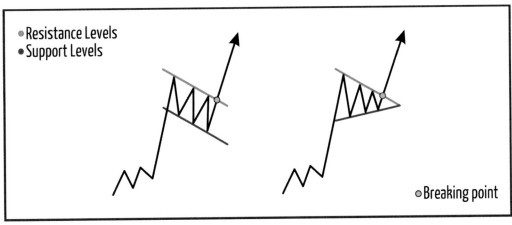

Figure 8.10 Flag and pennant pattern in an uptrend. In an upward continuation, the downward flag leads to less indecision than the pennant. The latter is a smaller replica of the symmetrical triangle which is a pattern of indecision that may lead the stock upwards or pulldown. Favor the flag in your search for an upward signal.

A downward flag in an upward continuation is perceived as a bullish signal and as an indication that the previous rising trend will continue. After a sudden and steep price climb, a flag reflects a temporary pause in the ascending trend, consisting of two parallel trend lines that draw the shape of a rectangular flag.

The flag has a downward trend which seems to go against the tide. Favor the flags that last between 12 and 20 days. A longer duration invalidates the pattern. Favor the upward breaks which are sustained by a steady volume.

Figure 8.11 Pfizer and bullish flag in an upward trend. Chart courtesy of StockCharts.com

The above figure illustrates a downward flag in an upward continuation. Some investors had sold when the stock began its decline in the early part of December. However, new investors accumulate, hoping it will rise further.

As the symmetrical triangle, the pennant is a wavering pattern that is built with two converging lines, one for support and the other serving as resistance. After a sudden increase and price accentuation, a pennant reflects a temporary pause in the upward trend. Favor the pennants with durations of 20 days or fewer. After this period, we direct ourselves towards a symmetrical triangle whose trend, upwards or downwards, often remains unpredictable.

Figure 8.12 China Sunergy and bullish pennant. Chart courtesy of StockCharts.com

The above figure illustrates a pennant in an ascending continuation for China Sunergy. Note the volume increase is well superior to the days that precede the upward break of the resistance. The sudden volume rise adds more vigor to the increase of the stock price, which doubled in two weeks. This increase in volume suggests another leg of growth starting in late October 2013.

Flag and Pennant Bear Pattern

The upward flag and pennant are patterns found during a downward trend. The fall happens in two phases interrupted by a momentary pause. The sharp drop is often caused by bad news referring to the stock. This transition period is marked by a lower volume just before the stock flies on higher volumes.

You should know that these different models are not 100 percent guaranteed. The patterns could get destroyed at the midpoint of their realization. Some economic news, the arrival of further investors or technology improvement by a competitor could influence the stock price. Technical analysis cannot predict all external variables to the share. You must be well aware!

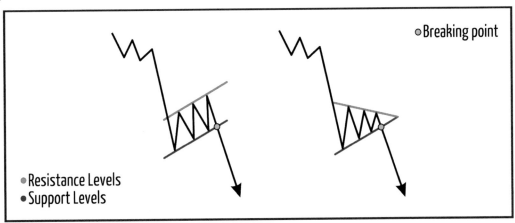

Figure 8.13 Flag and pennant pattern in a downtrend. The downward flag in an upward continuation provides less indecision as the pennant. The latter is a smaller replica of the symmetrical triangle, which is an indecision pattern.

An upward flag in a declining continuation is perceived as a bearish signal and as an indication that the previous downward trend will continue. After a steep descent of the stock price, a flag reflects a temporary pause in the sliding trend, consisting of two parallel trend lines that form a rectangular flag. This flag has an upward trend that seems to go against the wave. Favor the flags that last 20 days or less. Past this time, the pattern is invalid.

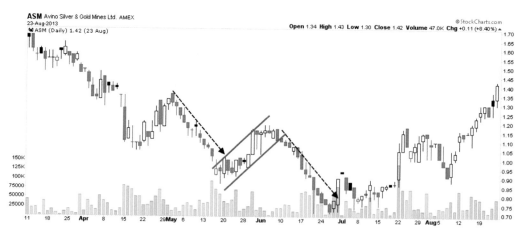

Figure 8.14 Avino Silver & Gold Mines and bearish flag. This figure shows a downward trend of Avino Silver from May to July 2013, broken by a bullish flag. Note the symmetry of the slumps identified through the black arrows. Chart courtesy of StockCharts.com

Bearish or Rising Wedge

The rising wedge in a downtrend lays the premises of a new low level. The trading range may take several periods and is characterized by higher highs and higher lows and a decrease of the transaction volumes. Consequently, the second decline begins without the backing of an increase of the volume of the transactions.

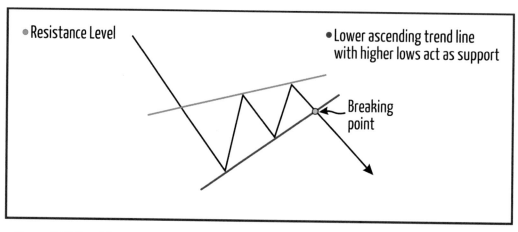

Figure 8.15 Bearish or rising wedge. The rising wedge allows anticipating a downward break of a stock. The top and the base of the triangle should be traced by joining at least three candlesticks so that the formation would be recognized as valid. The volume increase on the downward break is not required.

The length of the decline before the formation of the triangle is typically used to anticipate the duration of the second decline. The symmetry between the two drops is quite common. The example from 8.16 illustrates the beautiful downtrend, the break, and the second phase of the decline of the stock. Note the lack of the apparent rise of the volume in the fall of the stock.

Figure 8.16 STR Holdings and rising wedge. Chart courtesy of StockCharts.com

Bullish or Falling Wedge

A falling wedge usually marks a pause in an uptrend, but we also find it in a trend reversal pattern. The stock leaps within a corridor dominated by support and resistance. The corridor has the shape of a triangle with the slope oriented towards the bottom. The contraction of the triangle's extremity announces the future break of a stock. A consensus emerged between the buyers and sellers before the upward trend came back even stronger.

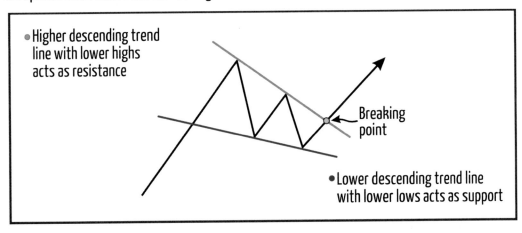

Figure 8.17 Bullish or falling wedge. The falling wedge allows anticipating an upward break of the stock. The break on high volume is required and reassures the investors.

The length of the leg before the formation of the triangle is used to anticipate the length of the second rise. Symmetry between the two increases is quite frequent. However, the increase could present small traps, and the rise will not necessarily be made in a straight line.

Figure 8.18 YRC Worldwide & falling wedge. Chart courtesy of StockCharts.com

The above chart illustrates beautifully that the ascension of the YRC Worldwide is made in two sequences, interspersed by a descending wedge. The latter allows future investors to make a stand. Note the increase in volume on the wedge breakout.

CHAPTER 9 – REVERSAL PATTERNS

We can never repeat enough the importance of drawing some trend lines above and below the candlesticks. It is possible to detect patterns without any calculations. Reversal patterns are numerous, but we will focus on the most popular. Don't forget that these patterns apply to stock market indices and sectors.

The most popular figures are the bump and run reversal bottom and top, the double top and double bottom, the triple top and triple bottom, the head and shoulders pattern, the rounding bottom and the parabolic rise. These figures are easy to identify and can even be spotted by tools available on the web or from your brokerage firm.

The reversal patterns often have a higher efficiency than the continuation patterns. It is easier to anticipate the buy or sell signal on these kinds of figures. Be on the lookout, as these patterns could generate important gains. Pay attention to the weekly patterns; potential gains will be greater than the stocks identified on a daily chart.

Bump and Run Bottom Reversal

The bump and run bottom reversal is a pattern that announces an upward trend reversal of a stock or index. It is characterized by a soft-angled decline followed by a more rapid drop in share price. Consequently, the stock will reach an extreme low, consolidate its position and come back in power. We could observe a type of V- or U-shape. The buy signal is confirmed by a rising break of the meeting point between the first slope and the recent upward line.

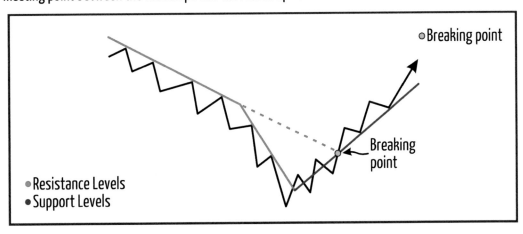

Figure 9.1 The bump and run bottom reversal is an upward reversal pattern characterized by two types of decline; a moderated one and an accelerated one. It gives the investors all the time necessary to be well positioned. Purchase target can be anticipated a few periods in advance.

When the stock accelerates its decline, we could already prepare ourselves to monitor the reversal threshold closely. Consequently, simply wait for the break signal to invest in the stock. This pattern has been recognized by Thomas Bulkowski and was originally named Bump and Run Formation (BARF).

Figure 9.2 James River Coal & bump and run bottom reversal. Chart courtesy of StockCharts.com

The above figure presents the chart of James River Coal. The bump and run bottom reversal pattern extends over a period of six months. The figure, although complex at first glance, shows the downward spiral of the stock, its agony and its resurrection. Notice the buy signal generated in early May 2013. Investors who spotted this buy signal got very substantial profits. Backing of the volume on the rise of the stock is unequivocal.

Bump and Run Top Reversal

The bump and run top reversal is a pattern that announces a reversal. It is characterized by a moderate angle increase, followed by a steeper rise in the share price. Consequently, the stock will reach an extreme summit, consolidate its position and make a downward reversal.

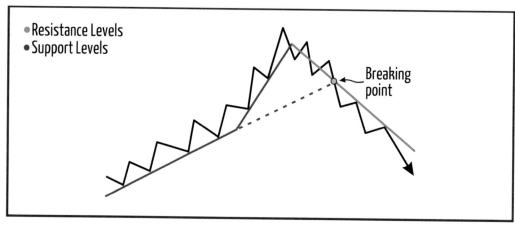

Figure 9.3 Bump and run top reversal. This pattern is characterized by two types of rising: a moderated one and an accelerated one. For the short-selling specialists, this is one of the greatest patterns. We could start preparing ourselves for a rapid descent to compensate for the unrestrained increase that the stock has just been through.

It looks like a reverse pattern of a V- or U-type. The sell signal is confirmed by the downward break of the meeting point between the first rising slope and the recent bottom line. This configuration often appears when stocks are in an uptrend and an alarm suddenly leads investors to invest in bulk. The final climb is more pronounced, or even parabolic, and usually announces an imminent collapse.

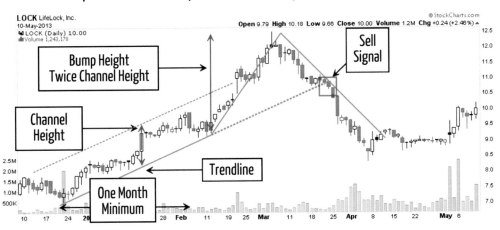

Figure 9.4 LifeLock & bump and Run Top Reversal. Chart courtesy of StockCharts.com

Double and Triple Bottom

The double bottom is a succession of two peaks of the same amplitude, offering a certain symmetry. This pattern takes the shape of a W. Lower reversal points represent the support zone or neckline. Stock price bounces twice on this support and suggests a trend reversal.

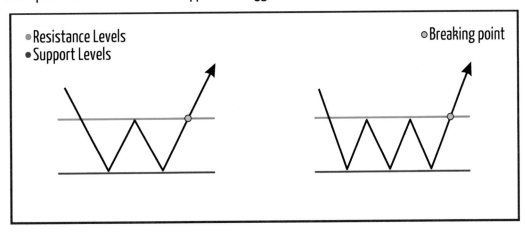

Figure 9.5 Double bottom. The double bottom is a reversal pattern that occurs after a downtrend and that extends over many periods (50 to 100). The pattern is confirmed by the break of the resistance line on heavy volume. The potential target is determined by adding the height of the W to the resistance line.

Bad news related to the stock or industry sector can explain the drop. After a long fall, the price forms a major bottom. Consequently, the stock makes a midterm retrenchment. Support and resistance lines are taking shape. Several investors take advantage to sell, after losing faith in the stock, and the share price falls to the same level as the previous low. After completing the second bottom, the stock goes back up, breaks through the resistance line and follows its growth.

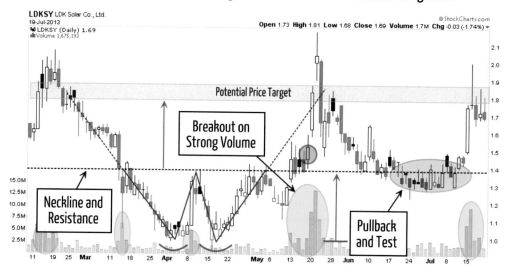

Figure 9.6 LDK Solar & double bottom. Chart courtesy of StockCharts.com

The above chart shows LDK Solar during a double bottom. Notice how the height of W under the neckline is similar to the gap between the neckline and the potential target. Don't hesitate to cash in your profits. Notice how quickly the stock retraced this path at the end of May. In June, the neckline was tested again, and the support was able to resist many attacks by traders. Furthermore, note the volume increase when the stock price reached the resistance, support or the potential target. The triple top is much rarer than the double top, but has similar characteristics.

Double and Triple Top

The double top is a downward reversal pattern. This model takes the shape of the letter M. The inability to cross a higher level can be seen, caused by a major resistance area. The pattern shows two peaks, roughly symmetrical with respect to the duration and amplitude.

After the first leg of the rise, the investors cash in their profits, and the stock drops in the intermediate zone. It will be followed by a rebound, which will form the support line. A second rise comes up against resistance. There are more sellers than buyers. The trend reversal is taking place. The stock continues to fall and breaks its support area. A sell signal is given, and the stock pursues its decline. A certain panic arises. The final target of the decline will be equal to twice the amplitude between the resistance and the support zones.

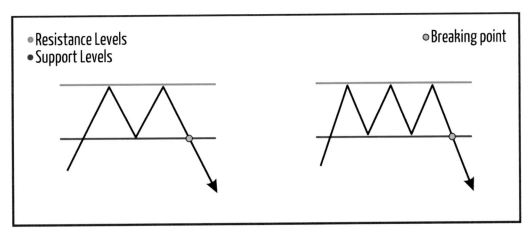

Figure 9.7 The double top is a reversal that occurs following an uptrend that spans many periods (50 to 100). The figure is confirmed on the breakdown of the support line. The potential target is determined by subtracting the height of the M to the support line.

Double top patterns are very common in stock charts. They can be recognized in different periods (hours, days, weeks). Pull your support and resistance lines in order to anticipate your operations.

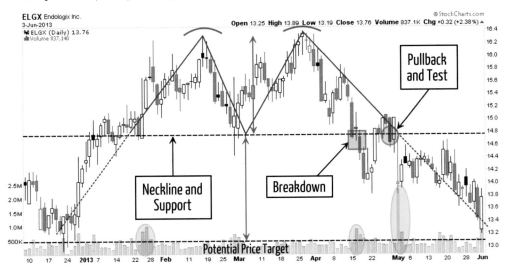

Figure 9.8 Endologix & double Top. Chart courtesy of StockCharts.com

The figure above shows the Endologix stock and the formation of the double top. A resistance zone prevents the stock price from moving forward twice. The first correction will determine the neckline and temporary support. Consequently, the stock price goes back and tests the resistance zone. This configuration strengthens the validity of the pattern because it reflects a lack of buyers. A second correction will occur, and the downward reversal will be validated by the neckline break.

Head and Shoulders Top

The head and shoulders top is a pattern found quite often and it's valued by many technicians. Its accuracy is quite disconcerting. This pattern suggests a downward trend reversal and resembles the top of a human body: head, shoulders and torso. It is recommended that you use this model in a weekly format.

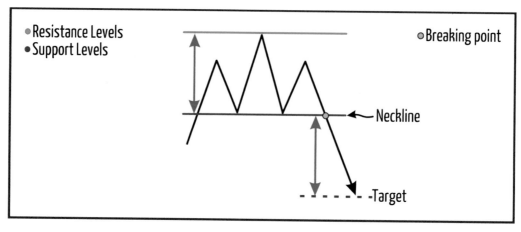

Figure 9.9 The head and shoulders top is a trend reversal pattern formed by three peaks. We can already anticipate the pattern during the head formation. An increase in volume is present during the formation of each peak. The neckline is tested three times. Not believing in bounces anymore, the buyers abandon the stock, which will eventually break the neckline.

The pattern takes shape in five steps:

Step 1
The left shoulder is formed by the first peak, followed by a decline that helps generate the neckline.

Step 2
The head is represented by a higher peak, followed by a decline that also comes to rely on the neckline.

Step 3
Consequently, there is the formation of the right shoulder. Give some importance to the symmetry of the shoulders, both in height and width. Some purists require a perfect symmetry of the shoulders. This requirement ensures that this pattern would be virtually non-existent and so useless in terms of learning.

Step 4
Always look out for a false breaking signal. It occurs when a candlestick closes below the neckline.

Step 5

In many cases, the height of the drop following the neckline break should be equivalent to the distance between the head and the neckline.

The figure below shows the potential target of Walter Energy stock. Note the symmetry of the length of the model. The figure took almost three years to build. The gap between the head and the neckline is $80. To establish the potential target, simply subtract the difference of $80 to the neckline value. In this case, we have a potentially negative target of $20 (or $60 minus $80). This is impossible, of course.

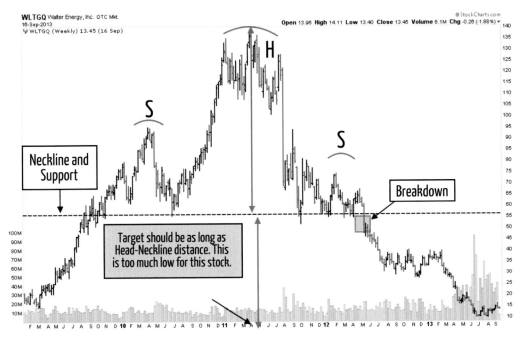

Figure 9.10 Walter Energy & head and shoulders top. Chart courtesy of StockCharts.com

This pattern is very appreciated by the short-sale specialists because the breaking of the neckline marks the absence of the support, mainly caused by the long-term pattern. Many buyers of 2008-2009 left the ship a long time ago.

Head and Shoulders Bottom

The inverse head and shoulders pattern, or head and shoulders bottom, is the inverse figure of the head and shoulders top. This pattern is a trend reversal made through three successive bottoms. Head and shoulders bottom resembles the upper body of a man, but reversed at 180 degrees. This pattern confirms an upward trend on the neckline break. It's particularly efficient in a weekly format, which is excellent for long-term investors.

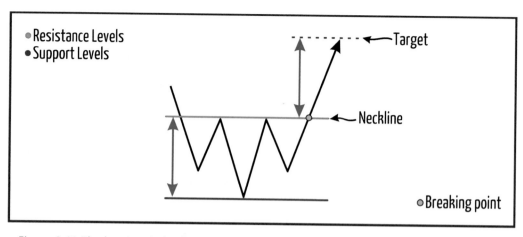

Figure 9.11 The head and shoulders bottom pattern is one of the most efficient trend reversal patterns. It is formed by three successive bottoms, the center having the highest amplitude. The neckline (resistance) is tested three times and breaks under the pressure from buyers.

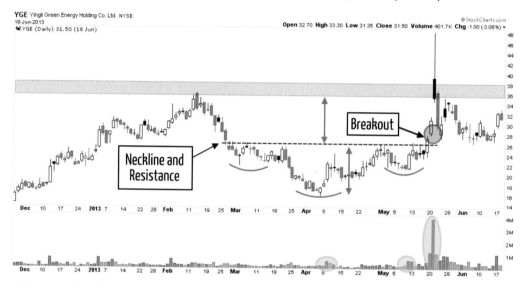

Figure 9.12 Yingli Green Holding & head and shoulders bottom. Chart courtesy of StockCharts.com

The figure above illustrates the head and shoulders bottom pattern for Yingli Green. The peaks reached between the different bottoms also build the neckline and the resistance. The neckline is not necessarily horizontal. The validity of this model is based on the strength of the break of the neckline. The breaking volume is the key factor to monitor. A break without a volume increase does not guarantee success.

Rounding Bottom

The rounding bottom is characterized by periodic low-volume transactions and small price differentials. To be valid, this pattern must extend a minimum of 20-25 periods. Even if it seems awfully difficult to follow, the rounding bottom pattern is one of the most explosive patterns.

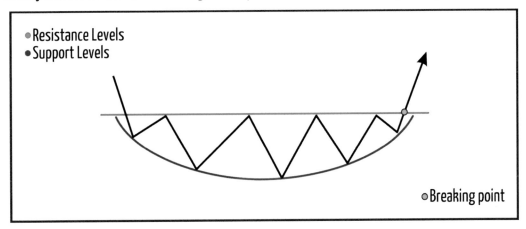

Figure 9.13 Rounding bottom pattern. Tired of following a stock whose price goes through a short amplitude corridor? You're making a big mistake. This model can lead to fabulous profits.

The stocks that have this type of pattern require investors who have a dose of extreme patience. This is an accumulation period. Place them on a watch list. Generally speaking, the longer the accumulation, the stronger the breakout will be once it occurs. There's no need to use mobile averages or other indicators, simply locate the resistance level and draw a line. Check the progress of each stock on a daily basis. Just wait for the break of the resistance line to take action.

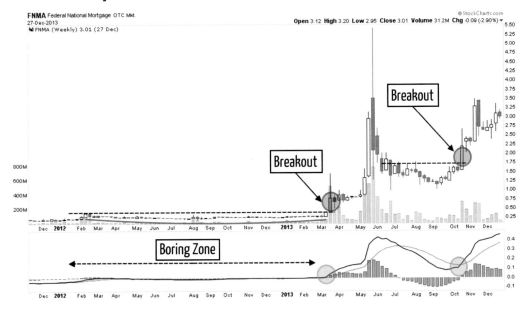

Figure 9.14 Federal National Mortgage & flat base. Chart courtesy of StockCharts.com

The Federal National Mortgage stock shows two rounding bottoms, the first being two times longer than the second. Your input is simple. Draw a horizontal line representing the resistance line and wait for the stock to break that line. The breakout of the resistance line has to be made on high volumes, as in every upward scenario. Notice the stock's volume in the background, during the first resistance line break.

The scenario is repeated again in 2013. The accumulation period was shorter, because the investors who missed the first bottom smelled the good deal and started accumulating stock in order to be ready for the second race. MACD was added, and it helps in decision-making. It clearly shows when to take action. When you see stocks in a consolidation period such as this one, you will know that you have to place them on a watch list in order to be ready for any eventuality.

The Parabolic Rise

As its name suggests, this figure illustrates the meteoric increase of a stock, in parabolic form. This pattern is caused by a high level of speculation. When you believe that the rise is complete, the acceleration of the increase continues even more beautifully. This type of movement valued by day traders is very difficult to manage for newbies.

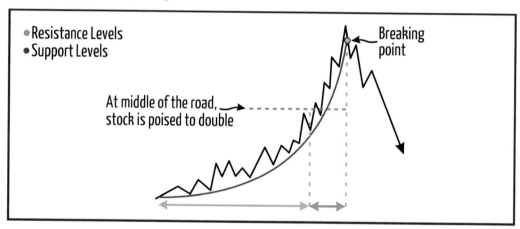

Figure 9.15 Parabolic rise. This pattern is similar to an arc of which the source is located on the horizontal axis and the end on the vertical axis. This model targets more often experienced traders who use short selling. The strategy is to wait for the downward break of the curve and sell short. The descent is usually much faster than the rising.

This model presents many traps, and it is often connected to securities with a high level of volatility. It is very difficult to anticipate the exit level. Tracking this pattern is delayed. It can be identified when it is at halfway. At this point, it is possible to draw an arc as a guide to expectations of an exit point.

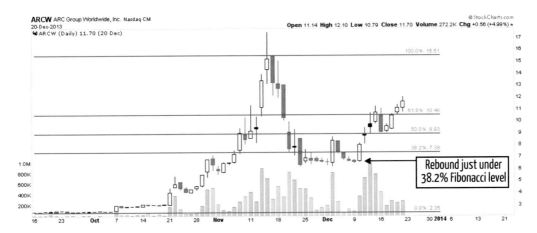

Figure 9.16 ARC Wireless solutions & parabolic rise. Chart courtesy of StockCharts.com

The above figure shows an exponential surge for Arc Wireless Solutions. In less than two months, the stock passed from $6 to $43.75. Completely amazing, folks! The stock seems to be supported by the arc traced on the base of the candlesticks. The downward break of the drawing sends out a sell signal. The professionals jubilate upon seeing this pattern and are positioning themselves to short sell, and cash fabulous profits.

CHAPTER 10 – CANDLESTICKS PATTERNS

As we saw in **Chapter 1**, the Japanese candlesticks represent in detail the price of a share for each period (minute, hour, day, week). Furthermore, as every technical indicator does, the candlesticks can equally generate trend reversal models or patterns useful for analyzing financial stocks.

When the time comes to make an investment decision, the candlesticks will not be enough. Do not see the candlesticks as a different way to analyze charts. You should rather see the candlesticks as a complement to the technical analysis. The candlesticks have to be combined with other indicators seen in previous chapters to maximize your investment decisions.

Use the candlesticks and its many configurations. Develop a routine of drawing your support and resistance lines, your corridors trend, triangles or other figures seen before. For example, during a double bottom pattern, pay attention to the presence of a candlestick that may announce an upward trend reversal. Closely monitor the support and resistance line breaks. The length of a candlestick measures the amplitude of the market's indecision.

Watch suits of candlesticks that have the same color. They announce a powerful signal of trend continuation. The combination of Japanese candlesticks and traditional technical analysis is the best way to consider all the strengths and weaknesses found in stocks. As this book is addressed to beginners, we will focus on the most important configurations. For those who want to perfect their knowledge, numerous works have already been written on this subject. Know that there are nearly one hundred different figures.

The use of these models must be combined with your favorite indicators in order to maximize your analysis. As technical indicators, the candlesticks do not allow you to predict the future. Good or bad economic news can bring a dramatic change in your outlook.

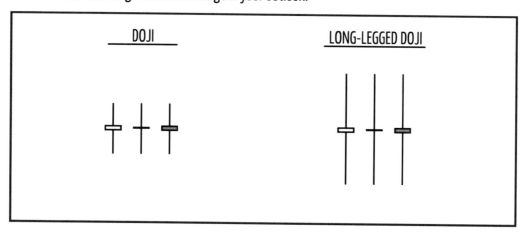

Figure 10.1 Doji and long-legged doji. Pattern type: Neutral. This candlestick presents average or long shades that indicate a neutral trend for the period. It marks a pause and could be the beginning of a new trend. If it comes to a support or resistance level, there is a good chance for a trend reversal.

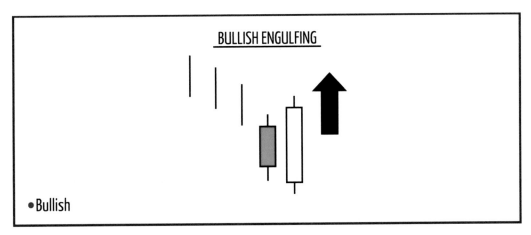

Figure 10.2 Bullish engulfing. Pattern type: Bullish. The bullish engulfing structure is a very efficient reversal pattern. It begins below the previous downward candlestick and ends its race above the same candlestick. There comes the engulfing pattern expression. The longer the candlestick is, the more powerful the engulfing structure will be.

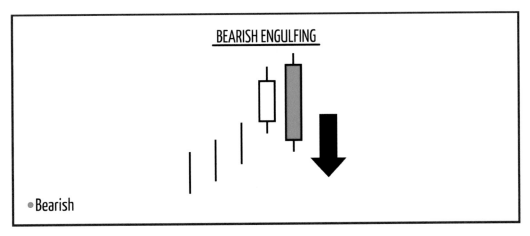

Figure 10.3 Bearish engulfing. Pattern type: Bearish. The bearish engulfing structure is a downtrend reversal pattern. Note that the downward engulfing must start above the previous upward candlestick and finish his race under the same candlestick. The longer the candlestick is, the significant more the generated signal.

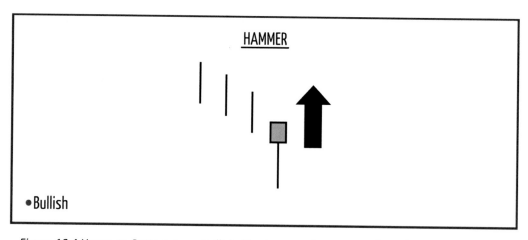

Figure 10.4 Hammer. Pattern type: Bullish. The hammer is an upward trend reversal pattern. The hammer knocks out the bottom. The elongated shadow indicates that the stock price has gone through a big selling pressure, but the session ended in strength and a positive way.

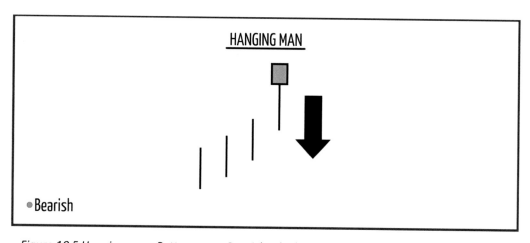

Figure 10.5 Hanging man. Pattern type: Bearish. The hanging man appears after an uptrend. The body of the candlestick should be small and preferably red (negative). The longer the downward shadow is, the stronger the reversal movement will be. The elongated shadow indicates that the stock price has gone through a significant selling pressure.

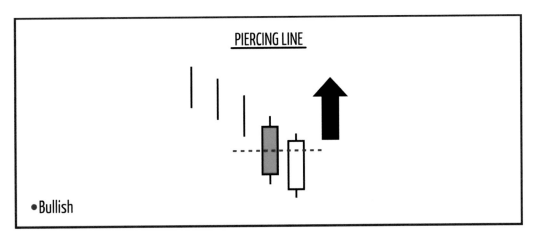

Figure 10.6 Piercing Line. Pattern Type: Bullish. The piercing line appears after a downtrend. It is a reversal pattern we find in the market's lows. You see a first red/black (negative) candlestick followed by a white/green (positive) candlestick that opens lower and manages to close above the middle of the previous red/black candlestick.

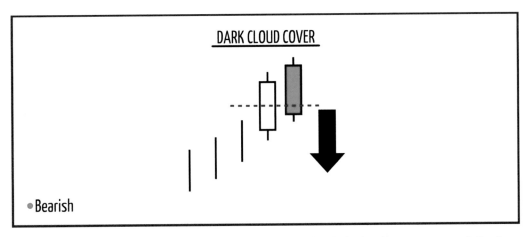

Figure 10.7 Dark Cloud Cover. Pattern type: Bearish. The dark cloud cover appears following a bullish trend. This is a reversal pattern we find in the market's highs. There is a first white/green (positive) candlestick, followed by a red/black candlestick that opens up higher and manages to close below the middle of the previous white/green candlestick.

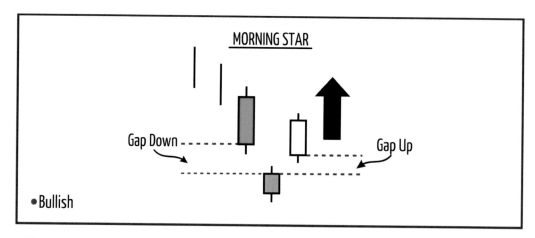

Figure 10.8 Morning Star. Type of pattern : Bullish. The morning star is represented by a doji or a candlestick with a small body (upward or downward), placed in a downtrend. We have to wait for the next upward candlestick to confirm the upward reversal. It is a reversal signal without great conviction.

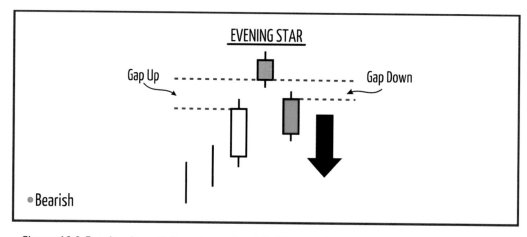

Figure 10.9 Evening Star. Pattern type: Bearish. The evening star is represented by a doji or a candlestick with a small body (upward or downward), which is located in an uptrend. The following bearish candlestick confirms the downward reversal. It is a sign of reversal without great conviction.

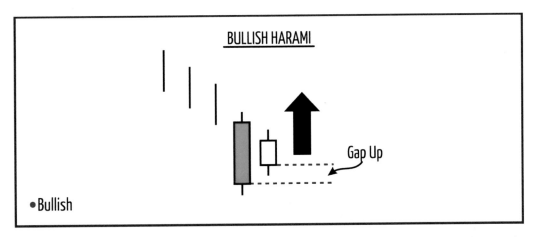

Figure 10.10 Bullish Harami. Pattern Type: Bullish. The small bullish candlestick begins the session with an upward gap. This candlestick is encompassed by the previous bearish (red or black) candlestick. The upward turn is confirmed if the next candlestick is up.

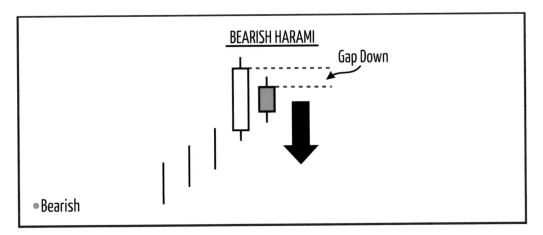

Figure 10.11 Bearish Harami. Pattern Type: Bearish. The small bearish candlestick begins the session with a downward gap. It is encompassed by the previous bullish candlestick. The downturn reversal has to be confirmed by another downward candlestick.

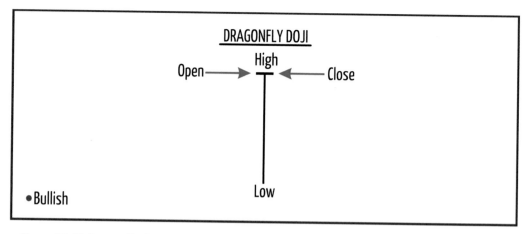

Figure 10.12 DragonFly Doji. Pattern Type: Bullish. This candlestick looks like the hammer and is the perfect candlestick in a bull market. Following the opening, a significant decrease occurred, but the market reversed. This allowed the stock to come back to its starting point. The longer the shade, the stronger the impact.

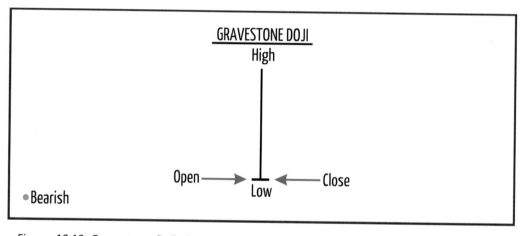

Figure 10.13 Gravestone Doji. Pattern Type: Bearish. This candlestick looks like an inverse hammer and represents the candlestick that nobody wants to see when invested in a bull market. This candlestick is formed when the opening and closing price are equal, and represents the low of the day. The long upper shadow suggests that the buying pressure of the day has been blocked by the sellers. It could be a major reversal.

Japanese candlesticks provide many configurations. Several financial tools provide the possibility to search for your favorite patterns. Your brokerage firm might offer such tools. Combine the candlestick patterns with the technical indicators and your analysis will be more precise. Learn how to spot these basic patterns quickly.

CHAPTER 11 – AVOID THE TRAPS

Technical analysis is a system whose efficiency is recognized. However, don't believe that this efficiency can reach 100 percent, especially since investors must cope with high-frequency trading. This trading mode is executed by specialized companies that have a huge advantage over small investors.

The best traders in the world have an efficiency rate of 80 to 90%. So, sooner or later, you will face an unexpected reversal. The idea of this chapter is to learn from your mistakes and avoid them in the future. There are many errors, most of them caused by our emotions, that can gradually consume our good judgment and our capital.

Fibonacci Retracement

The Fibonacci retracement is a very useful tool to extrapolate the amplitude of some movements. Retracements only serve to give potential targets. The basic principle is simple: At the end of a bull cycle with nice amplitude, you have to foresee the possibility of a pullback of 38.2%. Pay attention; the market forces can ensure a stock may decline by 50% or even 62.8%.

Here is the Fibonacci sequence presented in **Chapter 4**:

$$1, 1, 2, 3, 5, 8, 13, 21, 34, 55, 89, 144, 233...$$

Some financial providers do not offer the Fibonacci retracement tool. The tool shows the 38.2%, 50% and 61.8% retracements. The first ratio is calculated by dividing whichever number of the sequence by the second number that follows it. For example, 8/21 represents 38.09% and 13/34 results 38.23%. The third ratio of 61.8% is calculated by dividing any number of the sequence by the first following number. For example, 8/13 results in 61.54% and 13/21 results in 61.90%.

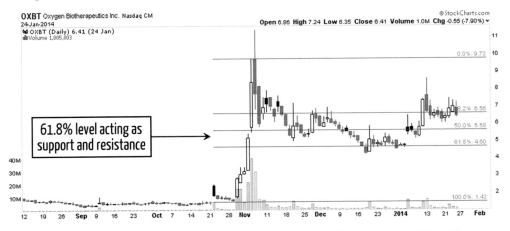

Figure 11.1 Oxygen Biotherapeutics & Fibonacci retracement. Chart courtesy of StockCharts.com

The figure 11.1 shows the pullback of Oxygen Biotherapeutics shares after having reached a new top in early November 2013. The decline has fully stopped at 61.8%, to bounce off the 50% level. However, don't believe that these levels act as magnets. Many investors watch these levels and act at the same time. The Fibonacci retracements help set targets and bounces. Use this tool for each bullish or bearish cycle; it will be helpful in your projections.

Fake Head and Shoulders

Take the time to analyze your stocks by including as many tools as possible in order to highlight signs of reversal or simply to watch for false signals. Do not only draw trend lines for the stock price, but also for indicators and volumes. Despite the potential power of a figure that emerges, a false signal could be generated.

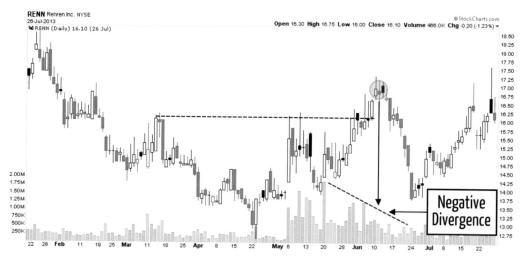

Figure 11.2 Renren & false head and shoulders bottom. Chart courtesy of StockCharts.com

The Renren stock featured a head and shoulders bottom pattern, merely a bit deformed, which didn't stop it from making a break higher than 10%. Two elements emerge from this chart. Firstly, the volume decrease since mid-May announced the failure of the neckline break. Secondly, the absence of a significant increase in volume on the break has stopped its momentum and has made it plunge more than 20% during June.

A divergence between volumes and the share price announced the breakout of the stock. A downward volume during a price increase cannot last for a long time. You don't need many indicators to analyze a figure; simple trend lines may be sufficient in many cases.

No Trend at All

The charts without trends and weak volume are lobster traps for the beginners. Unless you have the scoop of the century, avoid this kind of share at all costs. Quite often, these securities are registered in the secondary market, have some financial problems or do not respect the rules prescribed by the stock markets. We can count many "pump and dump" websites that use these penny stocks and artificially place overbids on stocks that are worthless.

Due to their low volume of transactions, the data connected to various indicators is of poor quality. You cannot have a reliable indicator. Avoid the gurus who make recommendations based on these types of stocks. It is nothing more than a lottery in which you have very little chance of winning.

Figure 11.3 Atlanticus Holdings – messy chart. Chart courtesy of StockCharts.com

You should avoid stocks that have a chart similar to the one of Nutrastar International. Its transaction average is less than 5,000 per day. Some days, there is no trading at all. Avoid traps that are presented to you and protect your assets from relevant variations.

Adjust Your Moving Averages

At some point in time, you will surely have the chance to see one of your stocks have an exponential boost in a few days. The most difficult thing for you to do would be to find the best selling point. To give you a small hand, reduce moving averages that you commonly use. The base junction created by two moving averages will launch a sell signal.

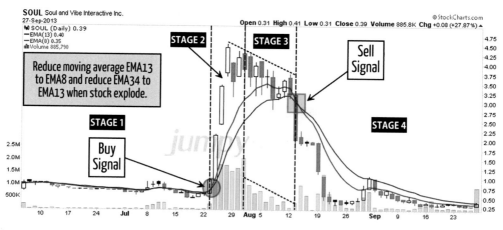

Figure 11.4 Soul and Vibe Interactive & moving average. Chart courtesy of StockCharts.com

Soul and Vibe Interactive presents the four stages of a stock in a daily format. As the rise was dazzling, you must use a lower moving average, such as an EMA8 combined with an EMA13, to detect a sell signal. A significant drop in volume in Stage 3 and the impossibility to stop its downward trend were sufficient to allow the stock to fall more than 30% in a single day. Notice the panic in volumes when crossing moving averages

Risky Symmetrical Triangle

The symmetrical triangle is a figure made of two lines opposed, with almost the same slope and whose meeting is manifested by a fall or a substantial increase. Unlike ascending or descending triangle, the symmetrical triangle announces a triangular indecision. It is very difficult to anticipate the type of break for this model. It was not until the very end to see the direction of the share price.

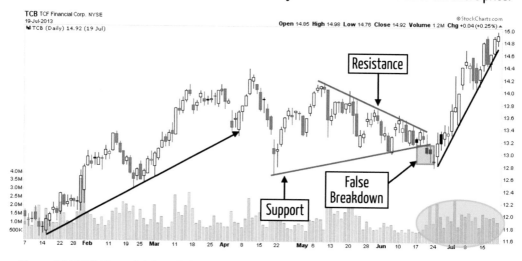

Figure 11.5 TCF Financial Corp & Symmetrical triangle. Chart courtesy of StockCharts.com

Symmetrical triangles are dangerous, because it is very difficult to foresee the direction that the stock might take. TCF Financial Corp has been in an uptrend since January 2013. The stock simulated a downward break at the exit of the triangle immediately to take off to a new high.

See how the volume increases in July 2013. Volume puts upward pressure on the stock. Do not waste time trying to anticipate the direction of the breakout for a symmetrical triangle. Before taking any action, wait until a real upside breakout.

Another Risky Symmetrical Triangle

Here is another example of a symmetrical triangle. The Investors Real Estate Trust has been in an uptrend since January 2013. The symmetrical triangle spans 40 days. The stock hit the superior bar of the triangle in late May and then broke its support.

Figure 11.6 Investors Real Estate Trust & symmetrical triangle. Chart courtesy of StockCharts.com

Nothing in the volume level provides an indication this stock will decline for a month. In addition, we have seen previously that the volume had less importance in a breakdown than during a breakout. If you used an EMA34, you would have gotten a sell signal just to the right side of the circle.

Super Rocket Stock

Quite often, some stocks have uncommon increases. Figure 11.7 presents the increase of Cleantech Solutions International, which more than doubled in late May 2013. Unless you're riveted to your screen, forget this type of pattern.

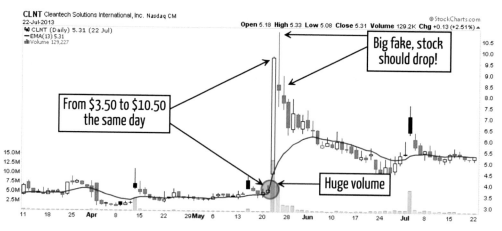

Figure 11.7 Cleantech & super rocket pattern. Chart courtesy of StockCharts.com

Notice the amazing volume compared to the volume of the other days. By chance, if you were positioned before that unthinkable growth, we hope you monitored your stock closely to collect wonderful profits. Nearly 15 million shares were traded in a single day, almost 100 times the average volume of the previous days. Social networks contribute greatly to the acceleration of the number of transactions. Good news spreads like wildfire. The pros accumulate solid gains and are getting ready for a short sale the next day. Several pump-and-dump websites lure amateurs with the promise of the following increase, but the fall suddenly happens. Many new traders enter this kind of situation and are royally devoured by the pros.

Long Candles & Long Shadows

New traders enter the market with a certain naivety. They hope for big gains, but the reality is poor. To clear their losses, these traders hope to find a guru that will grow their assets. When a guru recommends you to invest in a stock similar to Figure 11.8, run for your life! These stocks are traps that you must avoid at all costs.

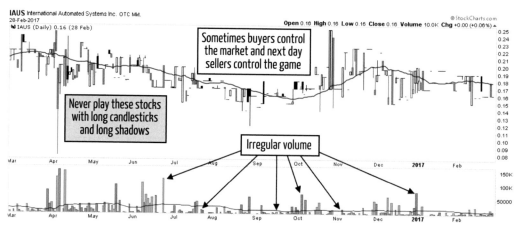

Figure 11.8 International automated Systems & long candles. Chart courtesy of StockCharts.com

The chart of International automated Systems one of the most beautiful traps a new investor could invest in. This stock does not show any particular trend. The candlesticks seem disordered, as if someone has tampered with the data. The long shadows of the candlesticks confirm unusual price gaps for most of the trading days.

In fact, there are days where buyers dominate and the next day, suddenly, the sellers are back in charge. It is impossible to find a bullish or bearish pattern that would allow investing in this kind of stock. Buyers and sellers cannot agree on a precise trend to give to the stock. The weak volume of transactions brings gaps between offer and demand. This type of distortion should be avoided. These charts often apply to companies with a small stock market capitalization. Avoid this kind of stock; there are hundreds of stocks that offer much greater potential.

CHAPTER 12 – PRELIMINARY ANALYSIS

This chapter presents some things to consider in order to properly plan the purchase of securities. Taking the time to invest in a stock does not only mean waiting for the ideal technical moment; other precautions are considered necessary before investing in a stock. Too many novices dive into a stock without taking the time to do some research about the targeted company.

Despite an extremely bullish chart, your stock could be on the way to presenting disastrous quarterly results. How do you prevent such a situation? Simply don't invest ahead of the announcement of the financial results! Take care of making your duties consciously in order to avoid falling into the many traps set by the pros.

1. Analyze the market and make sure the trend is positive.
- Check the market trend.
- Check the sector trend.
- Buy stock in a rising market.

2. Validate the recommendations made by your guru.
- Consider that the guru is ready to liquidate positions into strength even before you are invested.
- Consider only the selections made by the gurus whose securities are well supported by well-documented graphics.
- Do not chase any recommended stock that has won big percentage points in previous days.
- Avoid the traps from the discussion forums.
- Avoid the traps set by the "pump and dump" websites.

3. Study the company you want to invest in and/or the one that has been recommended to you.
- What is the profile of the company, what is its history? What is its integrity level? What are the main competitors?
- What is the date for the next financial results? Unless you are a soothsayer, never keep or buy a stock before the announcement of the quarterly results.
- What is the latest news concerning the company?

4. Strict trading rules to follow.
In order to avoid falling into the traps that the market makers could set, be careful and get ready for anything that may come your way.

- Before buying, establish your selling target. Limit your objectives for gaining.
- Never invest more than $2,000-$2,500 in one stock.
- Never invest in small companies rated as "pink sheet."

- Never chase the stock you want to have at all costs.
- Never hold more than three stocks at the same time.
- Never invest 100% of your assets.
- Never focus your acquisitions in the same sector.
- Never increase a losing position.
- Never invest in a stock without a clearly defined trend and not supported by a good volume.
- Never invest in a stock that has registered a massive decline after an amazing increase. The final rebound is impossible to forecast.
- Never fall in the day-trading trap – you will be quickly ruined!
- Never hesitate to sell a losing position.
- Never invest in the first 10-15 minutes after the market's opening. The stocks often make a quick increase, only to fall between 10:00 and 10:30.
- Never invest in stocks whose average daily volume for 30 days is less than 100,000 shares.

5. Trading psychology.

You have probably seen one of your friends losing control of his emotions before. Prepare yourself, because the trading world can make you go through all the existing emotions. Key points to remember:

- Never blindly trust your friends and gurus. Do your own research before trading.
- Remain modest; the market will remind you of this very quickly.
- Remain calm, and put your emotions aside.
- Never fall in love with a stock.
- Don't believe that you will make a profit in each of your transactions. Your success does not depend on the quality of your technical analysis. Rather, it depends on your capacity to manage your emotions.
- Take your profit when you can – you will not have a second chance.
- Be disciplined!

CHAPTER 13 – CONTROL YOUR EMOTIONS

The pressure experienced by a day trader is not comparable to that of long-term investor. The latter does not constantly examine his stock market portfolio. He rarely worries about his investments. In contrast, a trader is constantly under pressure. For many, the emotions take control and ruin numerous transactions. The best technician in the world has fewer chances of making profit than a trader who has full control of his emotions.

Take Control of Your Emotions

There's no doubt that this chapter is the most important one, even though it does not involve technical analysis. To make a profit in the stock markets, you need to discard emotions. The best way to do so is to develop a plan for each one of your trades. When you are in full trading action, take a moment and ask yourself if your emotions, good or bad, are going to dictate your way of trading.

- Did I buy because I received a scoop, or because I highlighted an excellent entry point by doing a stock analysis?
- Did I identify the levels of support and resistance of the coveted stock? Am I selling in a moment of panic?
- Did I collect information about the stock before buying it?

These simple questions will help you to plan your transactions and will protect you from making foolish decisions. The best traders in the world are primarily methodical investors who have very precise productivity objectives.

In the Heat of the Moment

To understand the different emotions that the beginner investor can go through, let's use a character. We'll call him Mr. Smith. Let's assume a situation similar to the one that many traders go through when they begin. Mr. Smith has no experience in trading, but wants to try his luck.

He goes to his financial institution to open a brokerage account. His brother-in-law gives him some advice for beginning in financial markets. Some websites provide background necessary to be ready to act. After a few days, Mr. Smith decides to take action and makes his first transaction. He invests in a stock proposed by a guru.

After two days, he notes with amazement that the stock already offers a 15% potential gain, thanks to a dazzling increase. He is very excited and can't believe how easy it can make money on the market. Mr. Smith goes through some euphoria. He truly believes that the surge will continue. It is not enough for him. Greed takes control, and he wants more. Subsequently, the stock stagnates and remains in a side corridor for a few days.

Mr. Smith asks himself if he should sell or keep the stock. He becomes worried, uneasy, and can't wait for a new leg up to start. He cannot believe that the increase is already over. The fear of losing a potential gain goes through his mind. Quickly, his stock falls and loses more than 20% just before the close of the markets. He is desperate to see that the situation has changed so radically, and decides to wait until the next day to see what happens. He hopes, and he is convinced that a reversal will occur sooner or later.

Mistake! The succeeding day, the stock continues its decline. Hastily, and without thinking during a panic crisis, Mr. Smith gives up and sells his stock with a loss of 35%. Totally discouraged, Mr. Smith is not proud of not having sold shares faster. He drops the market for now, completely stunned by his first experience.

Time goes by. He tries to understand what happened. He starts to follow the market again and doing research on the net to find websites that give good tips. When he spots a financial blog that gives scoops on stocks that have already registered gains of more than 100%, hope comes back.

The Market Emotions Cycle

Mr. Smith has gone through many emotions that made him lose control of his one and only stock. Sometimes positive, sometimes negative, emotions have taken control of his trading, making it impossible for him to know how to react in an unexpected situation. Here is the figure that presents the list of emotions lived by a trader, in connection with the four stages of the financial markets presented in **Chapter 2**.

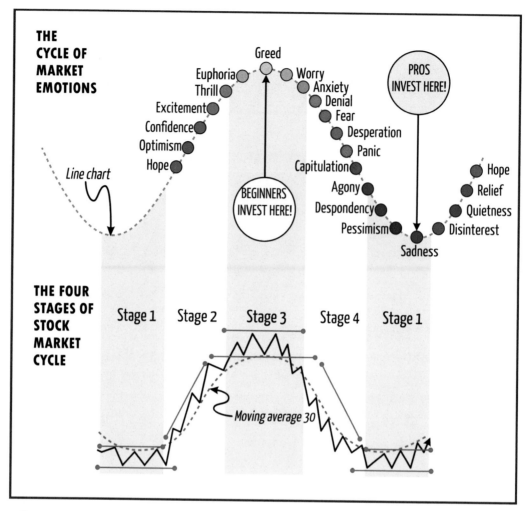

Figure 13.1 Market emotions cycle vs. stock market cycle. Chart courtesy of JumpyStocks.com

The above figure presents the superposition of two illustrations: The market emotions cycle and the four stages of the stock market cycle. This figure shows the relationship between the emotional cycle and the four stages of the financial market. The first one shows emotions lived by the traders, in connection with the bullish and bearish cycles of a share presented in the lower part.

This list is not exhaustive; it just gives an overview of the emotional cycles. Furthermore, observe that the time to invest is completely opposite whether you are a professional or a newbie stock picker. Professionals buy when the beginner is set to sell. The beginner is ready to buy when the professional is about to sell.

Avoid Emotional Pitfalls

Avoid discussion forums where most of the people are there only to pump up their stocks without using any graphs or information to support their claims. Ignore interventions such as "Go Apple Go!"

or "My friend told me that this stock is going to explode!" or "Netflix is going to $600 by Halloween!". These interventions do not help your investment strategy, and nothing is better than the research you can do.

Use Twitter or StockTwits and make a list of the best traders on the web. Block access to morons who provide no content or those who are simply pumping their stocks. We can recognize them very quickly.

Moreover, avoid being under unnecessary pressure by becoming the guru of a colleague or a friend. Otherwise, you will suffer from the fear of disappointing those who trust you. Imagine the face of your friend after a 20% decrease on a stock you had recommended. Avoid this kind of pressure that will ruin your analysis.

Avoid buying when the markets are falling. The market is always right, and you will eventually learn it brutally. Avoid the pressure to swim against the tide. Technical analysis is not an exact science. Furthermore, your stock may have the most beautiful upward pattern, but if the market is decreasing, your stock will also drop.

Be Disciplined

The best technical analysis is worthless when discipline and rigor are missing from your trading style. Stick to your initial plan and avoid the traps set by the financial community. Determine support and resistance lines to predict future events better. Learn to anticipate reversals. Stop being excessive! Remove from your vocabulary the words euphoria, greed, fear and hope. Replace them with more pragmatic terms such as analysis, plan or method.

You must be disciplined in performing your technical analysis as well as during the purchase of your stocks. Learn to limit your goals. Bet on small profits on a steady basis. Learn to cut short and take your losses. Admit your mistakes quickly and move on to another transaction. When the market is going through a bad period, the best option is to stay away.

When you have full control of your trading system, stay in a familiar field. Don't try new experiences. If you are successful, continue to work in the same type of market stocks. Be consistent; the small and frequent gains will shape your trading style. Forget gains of 15-25%. Base your strategy on real objectives.

CHAPTER 14 – STOCK TRADING TYPES

Whatever the type of trading used, it is important to have a good action plan to take control of your operations. You must put your emotions aside; they are the worst guide when it comes time to trade financial securities. Profitability starts with a good plan to help you determine the choice to buy or sell in the coming months.

Be methodical and structured. Refine your search tools to beat the market and get the best opportunities before anyone else. That is the secret. Taking action before the crowd increases your gains and your confidence level.

Technical analysis is the basis for an investor who wants to rely on something concrete before engaging in market speculation. Experience, either good or bad, will shape your trading style. Let's look at the most popular types of trading.

Day Trading

We are not trying to discourage you, but be aware that close to 90% of people who engage in day trading lose money. Day trading demands nerves of steel, foolproof concentration, and requires you to be riveted to your screen all day long. The day trader goes back and forth rapidly in the market, conserving positions for a few minutes to a few hours during the same trading session.

Day trading includes momentum trading, pattern trading, and scalping trading. These three forms of trading base their strategies on the anticipation of movements in connection with patterns and indicators. They search for the stocks that move significantly, with unusual volumes. Many professional traders use only the volume and the share price to trade. When we think about it, the indicators are derived from the share price and the volume to which it associates to different variables.

Swing Trading

Swing trading consists in buying low and selling high in an uptrend. During a downtrend, the objective consists of short selling at a high price and buying it back at a low. Many people associate this type of trading with trading short-term, only keeping a stock for a few hours or days. The purists do not like this association. The most important thing is to find the type of trading that will work best with your lifestyle.

Investors take advantage of all the dynamics provide by a stock, and they do not hesitate to sell when the market fluctuations signal a trend reversal. Swing trading requires methodology as well as rigorous research to identify clearly explosive stocks.

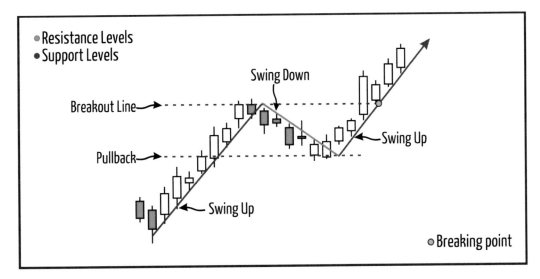

Figure 14.1 Swing trading.

Buy and Hold Strategy

This approach is quite simple: you buy, and you keep the stock for a few years. The strategy is based on the fundamental analysis of securities and requires no work. Just wait and hope you'll invest in a future APPLE. While most stocks oscillate in cycles, there are some stocks that have dazzling increases over several years. For example, take a look at Microsoft Company. An investor who bought that stock in 2000 wouldn't have any gains 13 years later, other than the dividends paid to the shareholders.

How would you define a long-term position? It is a short-term investment that has gone wrong. In fact, that is the truth for many investors. Instead of accepting their losses, they prefer to keep the stock, hoping for a positive reversal. Imagine a market that performs while your stock remains stuck in a downtrend. Favor long-term investments with mutual fund portfolios.

For traders, this strategy is rejected with the back of his hand. The potential of non-appreciation over a long period is very high. The idea of losing a lot of great opportunities repels the traders who have some experience in the market.

What's the Best Strategy?

Forget the miracles promised by the investment gurus – there's no right answer. In fact, use the strategy that works the best. Throughout your experience, you will develop and improve your strategy. Ultimately, the optimal strategy is the one that brings profits and the one you are most comfortable with. You'll meet on the way many pretentious web gurus that will promise to sell the best trading system in the world. Imagine if the world joined their system – everybody would be rich. You, and only you, will find the best strategy, and personalize it with the different tools available.

CHAPTER 15 – ANALYSIS OF A STOCK

Now is the time to get down to business: technical analysis of a stock. It's essential to make a first analysis of the stock on a weekly format. Why? The weekly makes it easier to identify the stages of the stock. As we have mentioned before, it's best to focus on stocks that are at Stage 2 and, even better, at the beginning of Stage 2. A stock that presents a beginning of Phase 2 will allow the stock to climb during several weeks, giving you time to cash lucrative gains.

You should imagine like the masters. These people remain connected to their screens every day, and they do not hesitate to sell at the approach of resistance. Novices hope for a breakout that probably will not happen, at least not sooner. The chart configurations are unlimited. With the experience, you will develop your configurations. It is important to use many indicators from the four families of indicators seen in the previous chapters. Make sure you are using at least one or two per family.

Weekly Chart Settings

Here is one of the configurations used to maximize your selection of stocks. Feel free to use other indicators to confirm some divergences. It is practically impossible to obtain perfect coordination between all the indicators. However, for each indicator, we present the parameters and triggering elements to meet.

Indicators	Settings	Triggering Factors
EMA	13	The trends of the stock and the EMA13 are upward.
EMA	34	The trends of the stock and the EMA34 are upward. The crossing of the (fast) EMA13 above the (slow) EMA34 triggers the buy signal.
ADX	14	Favor an upward +DI that has just crossed the 20 level.
Parabolic SAR	0.02,0.2	The trend is upward and the SAR indicator is below the stock price.
MACD	12,26,9	Favor an upward MACD with bullish crossing below the zero level.
Full Stochastic	14,7,7	Favor a stochastic that had reached a trough, which has returned upward and has just crossed the 20 level.
RSI	14	Favor a RSI that had reached a trough, which has returned upward and has just crossed the 30 level.
Bollinger bands	20,2	Favor the Bollinger bands that have been in contraction mode for several weeks and are now about to expand.
Acc/Dist		Favor an Acc/Dist that had reached a trough and has returned upward.
Volume	30 weeks MA	Favor stocks whose average volume at 30 weeks is more than a million shares exchanged.

Figure 15.1 Weekly settings

How to Analyze a Weekly Chart

Draw trend lines, support and resistance. Identify the bottleneck areas and the future points of sale. Identify patterns and divergences on the chart. Favor only entries at the beginning of Stage 2. Don't forget that weekly Stage 2 can last several weeks or even months.

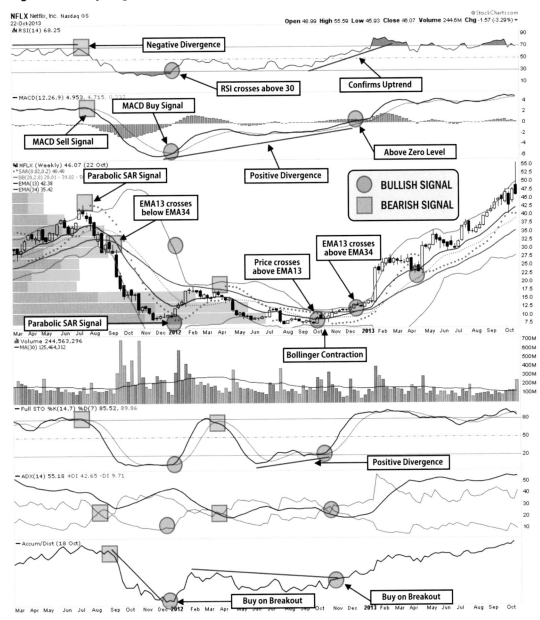

Figure 15.2 Weekly setup. Chart courtesy of StockCharts.com

101

Daily Chart Settings

Here is one of the configurations of daily charts. The analysis of the daily chart has only been useful to confirm the purchase already announced by the weekly chart.

Indicators	Settings	Triggering Factors
EMA	5	The trends of the stock and the EMA5 are upward.
EMA	13	The trends of the stock and the EMA13 are upward.
EMA	34	The crossing of the (fast) EMA13 above the (slow) EMA34 triggers the buy signal.
MA	50	The trend of the stock and the MA50 are upward. It represents a support zone for many investors during an increase.
MA	200	The MA200 is flattened or in a slight ascent. The very high gaps between the EMA13 and the MA200 remain unsustainable. A trend reversal is more than possible.
ADX	14	Pay attention to the trend reversal signal.
MACD	12,26,9	Pay attention to the trend reversal signal.
Full Stochastic	14,3,3	Pay attention at overbought and divergence signals.
RSI	14	Pay attention at overbought and divergence signals.
Bollinger bands	20,2	Favor the stocks on which Bollinger bands are in contraction mode for several days and are about to widen.
Volume	30 days moving average	Pay attention to the divergences between the stock price and volume. A drop in volume under the 30-day average indicates that buyers have lost enthusiasm for this stock.

Figure 15.3 Daiy settings

How to Analyze a Daily Chart

When comparing a daily chart with a weekly chart, notice that a buy signal (crossing of the EMA13 and the EMA34) is generated much earlier on the daily chart. There is a delay in the weekly signal compared to the signal generated by the daily chart. This is quite reasonable. If you convert an EMA13 and an EMA34 from a weekly to a daily format, you will obtain an EMA65 and an EMA170. Use these parameters on a daily chart. The crossing occurs in the same week as on the weekly chart when using an EMA13 and an EMA34.

The weekly chart served mainly to get a signal for buying. The daily chart is used to confirm the buy signal, but will also serve to get a cell signal. Draw trend lines, the support and resistance. Identify the bottleneck areas and the future sell points. Identify the patterns and divergences on the daily chart. From now on, you must check the conduct of your stock on the daily chart every day and spot the signs of weakness that could lead to the need to sell the share.

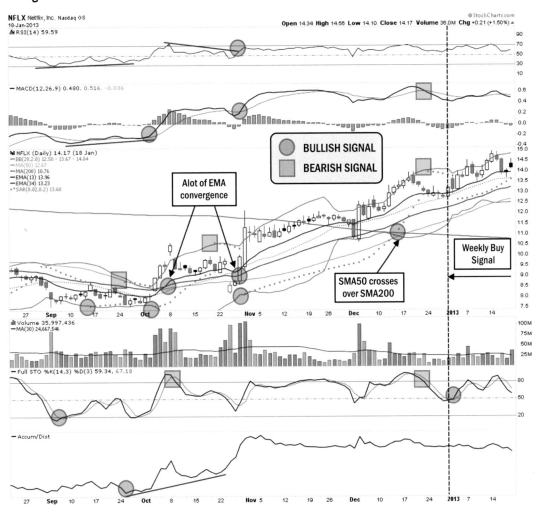

Figure 15.4 Daily setup. Chart courtesy of StockCharts.com

The above figure shows Netflix stock in a daily format. As you can see, many buy signals in daily setups were generated before the weekly signal, identified by the vertical dashed line. This is quite normal, since the periods in a daily format (days) are shorter than the periods in a weekly format (weeks). However, the weekly signals often have a longer duration.

The weekly signal is confirmed by a daily signal that happens at the same time. Observe that the weekly signal appears at an exchange rate of $92, while the first daily signal was triggered at $65. Do not hesitate to sell the stock on signs of weakness. Limit your performance goals. Small daily earnings will bring tremendous growth to your assets.

CHAPTER 16 – AN UPWARD DAY

To understand how the day goes by in the stock markets, use the intra-day chart of Twitter. Volumes are very high. Every day, several million shares are being exchanged. Twitter represents very well the ups and downs of a trading day. It is similar to many available stocks, regardless of the industry. A typical trading day is split into four different periods. Let's take a closer look at each of them.

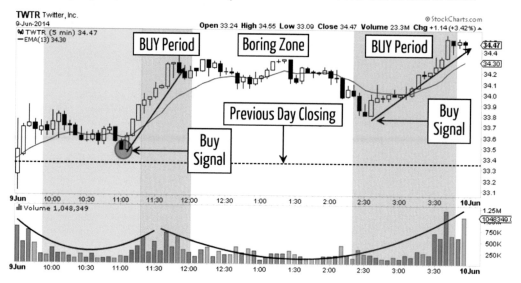

Figure 16.1 Intraday chart of Twitter. Chart courtesy of StockCharts.com

Period 1. Opening Markets.

This period is the most volatile of all. Quite often, the upward pressure is so high that it forms a gap at the opening of the markets. The increase continues in the first half hour. All orders accumulated during the night are being executed. This time favors a significant increase in the exchanged volume.

The highest gains are obtained during this short period. Gains varying from 2% to 5% are quite common, prompting traders to position the day before. Subsequently, the stock drops because the pros are cashing their profits very fast. Experience will teach you that a pro has little patience, and it is important to take profits quickly.

Period 2. Buy Zone.

The second period begins when the pullback is complete and lasts until the midday pause. This period still overflows with activity. This is the best time of the day to buy a stock. You will rarely swim against the tide because you bought cheaply.

Period 3. Boring Zone.

Most of this period happens during lunch hour. Many traders take a small break. Market makers are meeting to prepare the game plan for the afternoon. This zone is the least volatile of the day, with a much lower volume. This period is less attractive and offers a lesser possibility of gains.

Period 4. Buy Zone.

This last period is particularly interesting for taking positions. Many stocks were ending the day well and will start with a bang the next day. This period can favor an important volume increase and volatility level. Get used to moving yourself to the end of the day and enjoying the momentum. Unless there's bad news, the stock should open strongly the next day.

CHAPTER 17 – REGULAR ERRORS

Error 1. Underestimating the Market.

Whatever you may think, the markets are always right. The market cannot do anything about a stock that should increase instead of falling. The stock market is the crowd following actions set by the market's regulators.

Learn to act more quickly than others in order to maximize your gains and reduce your losses. Even if you disagree, the market sells on good news and buys on bad news. You must accept and implement this immediately.

Error 2. Not Limiting Your Losses.

You will lose money on a transaction at one time or another. You must accept it with humility. When a position does not turn in your advantage, sell the stock quickly. It is better to sell and invest in another stock than to allow yourself to be dragged in a loss that will take weeks to be cleared.

Do not hesitate to use a stop order. Most of the times, stop orders are used to limit a loss. If the shares you bought begin to depreciate, use a sell stop. If the shares that you sold short came to appreciate, use a buy stop.

Error 3. Not Making the Preliminary Analysis of the Stocks.

You must take time to analyze the coveted stocks, as shown in **Chapter 12**. The preliminary analysis allows you to reinforce your decisions and very often avoid investing in a bad stock. For example, investing before the announcement of the quarterly results can be catastrophic. Avoid putting yourself through irreversible situations.

Be proactive in your research. Never invest under the influence of emotion. Never blindly act on the options suggested by your financial guru. Always validate the choices suggested on the web, or in other places. Never push blindly for a trade.

Error 4. Investing against the Market's Trend.

Unless you master the short sale perfectly, avoid investing when the indices are going downward. Use the weekly charts and check the trends of the indices. A first alarm signal is sent when the index crosses below the EMA13. Many other indicators such as the MACD, ADX or the RSI send divergent signals. Pay attention to these signals and stay on the sidelines.

Instead, wait until the market turns upwards, and the index goes above the EMA13. The second confirmation signal will occur when the EMA13 passes above the EMA34. Be patient and stay disciplined!.

Error 5. Not Diversifying Investments.

Do not focus your purchases in a single industry. In the case of bad news, your portfolio could suffer a major drop. For example, negative quarterly results from an industry leader will certainly have an impact on its competitors.

You should diversify your investments because you cannot accurately predict future events. It reduces the impact of bad news in a particular sector. Simply don't place all eggs in the same basket.

Error 6. Living with Hope.

Hoping that a stock will gain 20% in a day or hoping that a stock will recover from a 25% loss is very unrealistic, even though that happens from time to time. Maybe this will happen one time in your life. Be pragmatic. Have realistic targets by choosing stocks that have well-defined trends.

If you live with hope, it is better to play the lottery or bingo. Take control of your investments. Start making good analysis and good research. Don't let yourself be at the mercy of your emotions.

CHAPTER 18 – STOCK MARKET GURUS

We must determine what a stock market guru is. The word "guru" is often associated with those prophets who claim to speak in the name of God. They attract many of the faithful on Sunday morning. Similarly, the stock market guru is a financial visionary, capable of detecting efficient shares. In our case, he is a specialist in stock-picking.

This type of guru is widespread on social networks. Cyberspace has permitted the emergence of many pseudo-specialists that offer their stock picks. Many sell their choice against an annual subscription, and others do it for free. Often, gurus hope to attract attention so that the wave of subscribers can influence the market.

Choosing a guru

As in sports, work or hobbies, many people need to have a person by their side who they can learn from, or a master who can reassure them when they're making decisions. It is the same for investment. Most people know nothing about investments and trust their bankers to help them choose the optimum investment. For many people, the best investment will be a bank deposit paying an interest rate of 1%.

First of all, don't mix up financial consultants working in a bank or brokerage firm with the guru specialist in selecting securities. The guru knows the financial markets well, and he has a flair for good picks. He works freely and is not forced to follow guidelines that may go against his values.

Dear investors, be careful, because you are easily attracted by the hope of quick profits. Avoid at all costs the gurus who only recommend investing in penny stocks. Penny stocks are even traded for fractions of a cent. They are often the target of promoters and manipulators. A promoter can create numerous websites whose mission will be to provide recommendations on the same financial stock and give the illusion that it is a future winner.

A simple trick: sign up to Twitter, use the search tool and type the acronym of the targeted penny stock. After a few attempts, you will find that different members have exactly the same list of recommendations. Their objective is to attract as many people as possible and catch some fish.

Many websites offer free recommendations for financial stocks. At first glance, this seems interesting. All you have to do is to provide an email address. Why provide an email address? Because they will take the opportunity to sell your address to other sites that work in the financial world. There is no reason to provide your email address in order to get free services. Protect your personal information and your privacy.

Other gurus will provide their picks for a monthly or annual subscription. The subscription costs between $500 and $1,500 yearly. Daily selections are available through several ways: a website, by email, SMS, Twitter or Facebook. The guru's choices will be ready for use before the daily opening of markets. It will be up to you to select the best of their choices.

Be Cautious about Gurus

Your most difficult task will be to find the best guru to fit your trading style and your aspirations. If you believe you've found a rare pearl, try the service for one month only. This will allow you to get an idea about the picks and information available. You will get an excellent overview of the returns it can get.

The selections of your guru must be supported by stock charts. This is a key element. Anyone can present himself as a stock market specialist and provide buy or sell recommendations. Those who support their picks by documented graphics have an edge over others. These professionals understand the importance of presenting picks supported by tangible elements such as technical indicators, bullish and bearish patterns, support and resistance lines, and divergences.

It will take a few days to see the quality of your guru's advice. Is his trading style fine with you? Does he sell stocks immediately after he recommends buying them? Does he buy on short or long term? Does he know the companies he recommended well? Does he make picks that follow the trend of the markets?

Don't take the gurus who make 15-20 recommendations per day too seriously. How are you supposed make the right choice among all their proposals? How do you track stocks with so many options? Don't trust this kind of guru. You must validate the proposed suggestions to avoid falling into traps. Logically, we like to invest in the stocks that have upward configurations with potential for a few days. Hence, the importance of knowing how to analyze securities.

CONCLUSION

I sincerely hope that this book will allow new investors to take control of their investments. Stop blindly trusting the advice of others and pay attention to the signals generated by the financial charts. Although the graphics cannot predict the future, it's still the only tangible support available. Avoid the pitfalls of stock markets. The best deal may be the one you do not do.

I wish you the best of luck!

Charles G. Koonitz

BIBLIOGRAPHY

Koonitz, Charles G. **Technical Analysis for Beginners** : Stop Blindly Following Stock Picks of Wall Street's Gurus and Learn Technical Analysis, Tripod Solutions, 162 pages, 2015. www.amazon.com/gp/product/B018TEKU12

Koonitz, Charles G. **Technical Analysis for Beginners Part Two** : Riding the Stock Market Cycle, Tripod Solutions, 125 pages, 2016. www.amazon.com/gp/product/ B01N65RDEI

Koonitz, Charles G. **Ebook Cover Design for Self-Publishers**: Create an Attractive Look Using Color, Typography, Pictures and Cover Design Concepts, Tripod Solutions, 158 pages, 2017. ww.amazon.com/gp/product/B018UGBAQI

Koonitz, Charles G. **99 Formatting Tips for Nonfiction eBooks**: How Format a Better eBook Using Various Tips on Cover Design, HTML, Typography, Images, Layout, Conversion and Testing, Tripod Solutions, 260 pages, 2017. ww.amazon.com/gp/product/B077GVTY8J

65983232R00062

Made in the USA
San Bernardino, CA
07 January 2018